Grammar

Form and Function 2A

Second Edition

WORKBOOK

Milada Broukal
Amy Parker

Mc
Graw
Hill

Grammar Form and Function, 2nd Edition 2A Workbook

English Adaptation 2011

Original ISBN: 978-0-07-301379-4

Editorial director: Tina B. Carver
Executive editor: Erik Gundersen
Sr. developmental editor: Annie Sullivan
Editorial assistant: Kasey Williamson
Production manager: MaryRose Bollwage
Cover design: Preface, Inc.
Interior design: Preface, Inc.
Art: Eldon Doty, Preface, Inc.

Photo credits:
All photos are courtesy of Getty Images Royalty-Free Collection, except p.91 Buzz Aldrin.
Page 91, view of Astronaut Edwin (Buzz) E. Aldrin Jr. in Lunar Module courtesy of NASA

2 3 4 5 6 7 8 9 30 Artec 20 25

When ordering this title, please use

ISBN 10: 89-6055-199-6
ISBN 13: 978-89-6055-199-2

Printed in Korea

Contents

UNIT 1 THE PRESENT

UNIT 2 THE PAST

UNIT 3 THE FUTURE

UNIT 4 NOUNS, ARTICLES, AND QUANTITY

UNIT 5 PRONOUNS

UNIT 6 THE PRESENT AND PAST PERFECT

UNIT 7 QUESTIONS AND PHRASAL VERBS

UNIT 1 THE PRESENT

1a The Simple Present: Statements

Student Book p. 2

1 Practice

Complete the sentences with the correct form of the verbs in parentheses. Make the verbs negative if the word *not* is in the parentheses.

1. Brendan (be) ______________ an actor.
2. He (work) ______________ in Hollywood.
3. He (not, be) ______________ famous.
4. He (not, make) ______________ a lot of money, but he (like) ______________ his job.
5. He (be) ______________ on a TV show. He (play) ______________ a college student.
6. Brendan (have) ______________ a girl friend.
7. Her name (be) ______________ Sheila. She (be) ______________ a dancer.
8. Sheila (not, eat) ______________ meat or junk food.
9. She (take) ______________ dance class on Saturday morning.
10. When she (not, have) ______________ a job dancing, she (work) ______________ in a restaurant.
11. They (not, live) ______________ together.
12. They (windsurf) ______________ almost every day.

2 Practice

Write the letter of the correct negative form in the blanks.

1. Jack __*d*__ married, and he __*c*__ have any children.
2. Domenic and Theresa ________ home now.
3. Claudia ________ watch TV.
4. I ________ have a large house because I ________ rich.
5. You ________ speak Korean, and I ________ speak Spanish.
6. Letitia ________ hungry, and we ________ thirsty now.
7. You ________ understand. I ________ angry. I'm just tired.
8. Mr. Phillips ________ wear glasses, and he ________ very young.

a. 'm not **b.** don't **c.** doesn't **d.** isn't **e.** aren't

3 Practice

Complete the sentences with the correct form of the verbs in parentheses.

Jackie: Debbie, who is this in the photo?

Debbie: Oh, that (be) ______*is*______ (1) my boyfriend.

Jackie: What's he like?

Debbie: He (be) __________ (2) fun. His name (be) __________ (3) Mark. He (be) __________ (4) really interesting. He (live) __________ (5) in Seattle and (teach) __________ (6) at a small college there. He (be) __________ (7) 31. He (have) __________ (8) brown eyes, and he (not, have) __________ (9) a lot of hair. I (think) __________ (10) he (be) __________ (11) really good looking.

He (not, have) __________ (12) a car, so he (ride) __________ (13) a bike to work. He (fly) __________ (14) to St. Louis every year to visit his dad. He (go) __________ (15) on ski trips every winter with his friends. We both (enjoy) __________ (16) music. We (call) __________ (17) each other often, and we (talk) __________ (18) for an hour. I (be) __________ (19) very happy.

4 Practice

Complete the sentences using an appropriate verb and the simple present tense.

1. Engineers *build bridges*.

2. A nurse ______________________.

3. Police officers ______________________.

4. A cook ______________________.

5. A president ______________________.

6. Students ______________________.

7. A photographer ______________________.

8. Birds ______________________.

9. A pilot ______________________.

10. A reporter ______________________.

1b Adverbs of Frequency

Student Book p. 6

5 Practice

Read the sentences about teenagers. Then rewrite the sentences and put the adverbs in the correct position.

1. Teenagers want to be independent.
   (usually) Teenagers usually want to be independent.
2. Parents worry about their children.
   (always) ______________________.
3. Teenagers go to bed before midnight.
   (rarely) ______________________.
4. Teenagers get part-time jobs.
   (sometimes) ______________________.
5. Parents want their children to be happy.
   (always) ______________________.
6. Teenagers tell their parents everything.
   (seldom) ______________________.
7. Parents are strict with their children.
   (often) ______________________.
8. Teenagers want to be with their friends.
   (always) ______________________.
9. Teenagers are interested in music.
   (usually) ______________________.
10. Parents disagree with their children.
    (sometimes) ______________________.
11. Teenagers are busy.
    (often) ______________________.
12. Parents stop loving their children.
    (never) ______________________.

6 Practice

Write about your parents.

1. My parents always ______________________________.

2. They rarely ______________________________.

3. They often ______________________________.

4. They're sometimes ______________________________.

5. They're not usually ______________________________.

6. They never ______________________________.

7 Practice

Adam and George are talking about a coworker. Put the adverbs in the correct position and use the correct form of the verbs in parentheses.

Adam: Laura (be, always) *is always* (1) early.

George: I know. And she (take, usually) ______ (2) only half an hour for lunch.

Adam: Yes. She (not, leave, often) ______ (3) early, and she (finish, always) ______ (4) her work.

George: It's amazing. She (call in, rarely) ______ (5) sick on Monday and (work, often) ______ (6) late.

Adam: She (be, usually) ______ (7) helpful to customers.

George: She (be, often) ______ (8) at her desk, and she (play, usually) ______ (9) music while she works.

Adam: And she (talk, never) ______ (10) to her friends on the phone.

George: Yeah, she's a really good worker.

8 Practice

Write about you and the people in your class. Use adverbs in your sentences.

1. *David always sits in the front.* (OR) *I'm rarely sick.*

2. ______________________________

3. ______________________________

4. ______________________________

5. ______________________________

6. ______________________________

7. ______________________________

8. ______________________________

9. ______________________________

10. ______________________________

1c The Present Progressive: Statements

Student Book p. 8

9 Practice

Write *C* next to the verb if it is spelled correctly. Write *I* if it is spelled incorrectly.

______ 1. beginning

______ 2. happenning

______ 3. shoping

______ 4. looking

______ 5. danceing

______ 6. running

______ 7. criing

______ 8. saying

______ 9. doing

______ 10. smelling

______ 11. eating

______ 12. liveing

10 Practice

Complete the sentences with the present progressive form of the verbs in parentheses.

A. Today is Fran's birthday. Her friends (plan) ______________ (1) a surprise party for her. They (wait) ______________ (2) for Fran to leave. Her friends (watch) ______________ (3) her from across the street.

Joe: What is she doing?

Marilyn: She (watch) ______________ (4) TV. Oh, now she (get up) ______________ (5). She (turn off) ______________ (6) the TV. She (put on) ______________ (7) her coat. Okay, she (leave) ______________ (8).

Joe: Good. Let's go. I have the key to her house. Who has the cake?

B. Ken: Where is everyone?

Mari: Well, Tammy (play) ____________ (1) soccer. Satchiko (shop) ____________ (2) for CDs with her friends, and Nicola (take) ____________ (3) a nap. I (make) ____________ (4) cookies.

C. Ben is on a business trip with two coworkers. He (talk) ____________ (1) to his friend Sarah on the phone.

Ben: Hi, Sarah.

Sarah: Hi! Are you having a good time?

Ben: Yeah, it's okay. Jerry and Eric (watch) ____________ (2) baseball, and we (eat) ____________ (3) some pizza right now. (*Ben sneezes.*)

Sarah: Are you okay?

Ben: Yeah, but I think I (get) ____________ (4) a cold.

D. A video (play) ____________ (1) in the living room. Angela (watch) ____________ (2) the video while Allison (make) ____________ (3) popcorn in the kitchen.

Allison: What's happening?

Angela: The girl (cry) ____________ (4), and the boy (hold) ____________ (5) her hand. Okay, now we (look) ____________ (6) at a house. A car (drive) ____________ (7) up. The girl (get out) ____________ (8) of the car and (run) ____________ (9) to the door.

Allison: Why?

Angela: I don't know! Come in here. You (miss) ____________ (10) everything!

II Practice

Answer the questions using the present progressive tense.

1. Look outside. What's happening? *A woman is riding a bicycle. Some children are playing basketball.*
2. How is the weather? ____________.
3. What is happening in your country now? ____________.

4. What's happening in the world? ______________________________.

5. What are your classmates doing? ______________________________.

12 Practice

Look at the photo. Write sentences using the present progressive tense.

1. ______________________________.
2. ______________________________.
3. ______________________________.
4. ______________________________.

1d The Simple Present OR The Present Progressive

Student Book p. 11

13 Practice

Complete the sentences. Use the simple present or the present progressive of the verbs in parentheses. Contractions or full forms are correct.

1. I (usually, make) ______________ coffee at 7:30, but today is Saturday!

   So, I (make) ______________ coffee now, even though it is 9:00.

2. On Thursdays, Vivian paints for two hours. Today, Vivian (not, paint)

   ______________ because she (not, feel) ______________ well.

3. **A:** What's Mickey doing?

   B: He (try) ______________ to stand on his head.

4. Jeff (usually, not, play) ______________ soccer, but he (play) ______________ soccer today. He (not, have) ______________ many friends, so he (try) ______________ to meet people.

14 Practice

Complete the sentences with the simple present or present progressive of the verbs in parentheses.

Many unusual animals (live) ______________ (1) in Australia, like the koala, the kangaroo, and the wallaby. Australia (have) ______________ (2) about 20 million people. The people (speak) ______________ (3) English, and they (use) ______________ (4) the Australian dollar. Today, more people (go) ______________ (5) to Australia, and tourism (grow) ______________ (6).

15 Practice

Complete the sentences with the simple present or present progressive of the verbs in parentheses.

Giant pandas (live) ______________ (1) only in China. They (eat) ______________ (2) bamboo and (usually, not make) ______________ (3) many sounds. They (like) ______________ (4) the cold, wet forests in China, and they only (have) ______________ (5) one baby a year. They (not, see) ______________ (6) well, and an adult male panda (weigh) ______________ (7) almost 300 pounds! But the giant panda (be) ______________ (8) in trouble. Today, the number of giant pandas (get) ______________ (9) smaller.

16 Practice

Read the sentences. Write *C* next to the sentence if the simple present or the present progressive is used correctly. Write *I* if it is used incorrectly.

_____ **1.** I'm always tired in the morning.

_____ **2.** I'm usually eating breakfast every day.

_____ **3.** People are speaking Portuguese in Brazil.

_____ **4.** Cesare drinks coffee every morning.

_____ **5.** Elizabeth is always talking now.

_____ **6.** Javier is looking out the window.

_____ **7.** Kimberly is always doing her homework at 7:00.

_____ **8.** Yiwen takes a shower now.

_____ **9.** Min is watching TV now.

_____ **10.** Eun Kyung rides her bike today.

1e Nonaction or Stative Verbs

Student Book p. 14

17 Practice

Read the letter and complete the sentences with the simple present or the present progressive tense.

Dear Hans,

How are you? I (be) _______________ (1) in science class right now, but we (take) _______________ (2) a break. I (like) _______________ (3) the class, but I (not, understand) _______________ (4) the teacher. She (speak, usually) _______________ (5) too fast.

My other classes (be) _______________ (6) fine, and I (know) _______________ (7) a lot of people now. I (not, have) _______________ (8) a lot of homework.

Oh, the teacher (start) _______________ (9) class again. I (think) _______________ (10) of you.

Bye,

Carole

18 Practice

Circle the letter of the correct sentence.

1. **a.** Lisa remembers me.
b. Lisa is remembering me.

2. **a.** I'm not knowing the answer.
b. I don't know the answer.

3. **a.** I'm hating math.
b. I hate math.

4. **a.** Debbie likes bowling.
b. Debbie is liking bowling.

5. **a.** Dinner is smelling good!
b. Dinner smells good!

1f *See, Look At, Watch, Hear,* and *Listen To*

Student Book p. 15

19 Practice

Read the following sentences. Underline the correct verb.

1. **A:** Tina is skating.
   B: Where is she? I (don't look at / don't see) her.
2. Tom, you (don't hear / 're not listening to) me!
3. Jay, please (see / look at) me when I'm talking to you.
4. There's the party. I (hear / listen to) music. It's at that house.
5. I wear glasses because I (don't see / am not looking at) well.
6. On Sunday afternoon, my uncles (watch / see) football.
7. Peggy is daydreaming. She isn't (listening to / hearing) the teacher.
8. A good babysitter (looks at / watches) children carefully.
9. **A:** What are you doing?
   B: I ('m seeing / 'm looking at) the garden.
10. Wake up. I ('m listening to / hear) the baby. She's crying.
11. Steven (doesn't see / doesn't watch) TV.
12. Do you (hear / listen to) the radio in the car?

20 Practice

Complete the sentences with *hear, listen to, watch, see,* or *look at.* Use the simple present or the present continuous tense.

1. Uma ____________________ MTV right now.
2. Tyler ____________________ music at night.
3. Ho Joon ____________________ the stars right now.
4. I'm scared. I ____________________ a noise in the kitchen. I don't know what it is.
5. The girls are home. I ____________________ them in the driveway getting out of the car.
6. Kiomi (not) ____________________ well. She wears contact lenses.

7. Todd (not) ____________________ at the blackboard. He ____________________ something outside.

8. My cousins ____________________ Spanish videos every Friday night.

9. Oh, I ____________________ birds outside. They're singing!

1g Yes/No Questions and Short Answers; Wh- Questions

Student Book p. 18

21 Practice

Write the letter of the correct short answer next to the question.

_____ 1. Do you work out in the morning?

_____ 2. Does your aunt live in Australia?

_____ 3. Are your parents coming with us?

_____ 4. Is it raining?

_____ 5. Are Ted and Jasmine having a party?

_____ 6. Is the water boiling?

_____ 7. Do you drive to work?

_____ 8. Does Kim take care of her mother?

a. Yes, they are.
b. Yes, she does.
c. No, I don't.
d. No, it isn't.

22 Practice

Write short answers to the questions.

1. Are you having fun? ____.

2. Do you ski? ____.

3. Are you listening to music? ____.

4. Do you speak French? ____.

5. Are you sitting in your bedroom? ____.

6. Are you working at your computer? ____.

7. Do you play an instrument? ____.

8. Are you interested in politics? ______________________________.

9. Do you have any pets? ______________________________.

10. Do you like English grammar? ______________________________.

11. Are you working hard? ______________________________.

12. Are you thinking about a snack? ______________________________.

23 Practice

Read the information. Then write questions and answers using the prompts.

Tigers are the largest animals in the cat family. Today, there are five different kinds of tigers in the world. Two of them are the Siberian tiger, which lives in eastern Russia, and the Bengal tiger, which lives in India. Siberian tigers are bigger than Bengal tigers because they live in a colder climate. They have thick fur and more fat under their skin. Male Siberian tigers sometimes weigh from 450 to 600 pounds.

Does your cat like to swim? Well, tigers do! Tigers also see very well at night, and they can eat 90 pounds of food at one time. Every tiger has a unique stripe pattern.

1. *Do Siberian tigers live in India?*
   No, they don't. They live in eastern Russia.

2. Where ______________________________?
   ______________________________.

3. Why ______________________________?
   ______________________________.

4. How much do ______________________________?
   ______________________________.

5. Do ______________________________?
   ______________________________.

24 Practice

Write questions and answers in the simple present or the present progressive using the prompts.

1. what/Burt/do/now *What is Burt doing now* ?

   fix/his car *He's fixing his car* .

2. who/go/store/with you ______?

   Ellen ______.

3. what/Martha/do______?

   she/be/a police officer ______.

4. when/you/take/a shower/in the morning ______?

   I/take/a shower/at 7:00 ______.

5. who/you/talk to ______?

   I/talk to/my sister ______.

6. what/you/think/about air pollution ______?

   I/think/it's a problem ______

7. what/you/think about ______?

   I/think about/lunch ______!

8. where/you/go/now ______?

   I/go/to the bank ______.

9. where/you/go on Sundays ______?

   I/go to/yoga class ______.

10. what/you/do ______?

    I/send/email ______.

SELF-TEST

A Choose the best answer, A, B, C, or D, to complete the sentence. Mark your answer by darkening the oval with the same letter.

1. Anita ________ smoke.

   A. is not (A) (B) (C) (D)
   B. doesn't
   C. is
   D. don't

2. It _______ in the summer.

   A. seldom rains (A) (B) (C) (D)
   B. rain
   C. isn't rain
   D. don't rain

3. Patty ________ in the garden now.

   A. don't work (A) (B) (C) (D)
   B. doesn't work
   C. works
   D. is working

4. I ________ you!

   A. remember (A) (B) (C) (D)
   B. am remembering
   C. is remembering
   D. am not remembering

5. Mrs. Kaufman ________ her new neighbor. She's not very friendly.

   A. isn't liking (A) (B) (C) (D)
   B. don't like
   C. like
   D. doesn't like

6. Gordon is at the museum this afternoon, and he ________ the new sculpture.

   A. is looking at (A) (B) (C) (D)
   B. see
   C. is watching
   D. is seeing

7. What ________ for dinner?

   A. is you wanting (A) (B) (C) (D)
   B. are you wanting
   C. does you wanting
   D. do you want

8. Fire ________ air, heat, and fuel.

   A. need (A) (B) (C) (D)
   B. needs
   C. is needing
   D. are needing

9. How much ________?

   A. do elephants weigh (A) (B) (C) (D)
   B. does elephants weigh
   C. are elephants weighing
   D. weigh elephants

10. My teenage children ________ tired in the evening.

    A. often is (A) (B) (C) (D)
    B. is often
    C. often are
    D. are often

B Find the underlined word or phrase, A, B, C, or D, that is incorrect. Mark your answer by darkening the oval with the same letter.

1. He usually (A) is (B) calls (C) his mother on Saturday mornings (D).

   (A) (B) (C) (D)

2. Sharon doesn't (A) speak (B) English, so she isn't understanding (C) what the newspapers (D) say.

   (A) (B) (C) (D)

3. Dogs usually (A) aren't (B) like (C) loud noises. Some dogs (D) run away.

   (A) (B) (C) (D)

4. Kevin is (A) usually (B) talking (C) to his children right now (D).

   (A) (B) (C) (D)

5. Kyle is listen to (A) music and playing (B) his guitar (C) right now (D).

   (A) (B) (C) (D)

6. Cats don't (A) flying (B). They also don't (C) like (D) to swim.

   (A) (B) (C) (D)

7. When do (A) they (B) usually going (C) to school (D)?

   (A) (B) (C) (D)

8. I'm (A) not having (B) a good time. I (C) go (D) home now.

   (A) (B) (C) (D)

9. The weather is (A) often (B) very pleasant in the fall. It (C) rains never (D) in the summer.

   (A) (B) (C) (D)

10. Michael (A) has (B) three brothers. He (C) isn't having (D) any sisters.

    (A) (B) (C) (D)

UNIT 2 THE PAST

2a The Simple Past

Student Book p. 28

1 Practice

Write *C* next to the past tense verb if it is spelled correctly. Write *I* if it is spelled incorrectly.

_______ **1.** fixed
_______ **2.** worryed
_______ **3.** exitted
_______ **4.** closed
_______ **5.** enjoied
_______ **6.** traveled
_______ **7.** planned
_______ **8.** visited
_______ **9.** cleanned
_______ **10.** stayed

2 Practice

Complete the sentences using the simple past tense of the verbs in parentheses.

Yesterday, I (need) _______(1) a cup of coffee, so I (walk) _______(2) to the coffee shop. The coffee shop is next to the bank. I (stop) _______(3) in front of the bank to buy a newspaper. Suddenly, the door (open) _______(4), and a man in a mask (look) _______(5) out. He (look) _______(6) at me and (shout) _______(7), "Get out of my way!" He (push) _______(8) me and (exit) _______(9) the bank quickly. I (start) _______(10) to follow him. I (grab) _______(11) his shoulder, and he (drop) _______(12) a bag of money from the bank. I (pull out) _______(13) my handcuffs and quickly (arrest) _______(14) him. I (call) _______(15) my partner, and she (arrive) _______(16) soon after that. The robber (try) _______(17) to escape, but we (push) _______(18) him into our car.

I am a police officer.

3 Practice

Write short answers to the questions.

1. Did you sleep well last night?

   Yes, I did. (OR) No, I didn't.

2. Did you read the newspaper yesterday?

   ______________________________.

3. Did your best friend call you last night?

   ______________________________.

4. Did a friend drive you to school last week?

   ______________________________.

5. Did you go on vacation last year?

   ______________________________.

6. Did you see any movies last weekend?

   ______________________________.

7. Did you use a computer today?

   ______________________________.

8. Did your parents teach you how to ride a bike when you were a child?

   ______________________________.

4 Practice

Write questions and answers using the prompts.

1. you/play/tennis last summer

   Did you play tennis last summer?

   Yes, I did. (OR) No, I didn't. I played basketball.

2. your teacher/give/you any homework today

   ______________________________?

   ______________________________.

3. you/understand/the lesson

______________________________?

______________________________.

4. your classmates/ask/questions in class

______________________________?

______________________________.

5. you/do/something special for your birthday last year

______________________________?

______________________________.

6. you/send/any email today

______________________________?

______________________________.

7. you/drive/anywhere this week

______________________________?

______________________________.

8. you/see/your best friend last weekend

______________________________?

______________________________.

9. you/study/for the last test

______________________________?

______________________________.

10. you/talk/to your neighbors last week

______________________________?

______________________________.

2b Irregular Verbs

Student Book p. 32

5 Practice

Write the present tense form of the following past tense verbs.

have **1.** had

_________ **2.** went

_________ **3.** sent

_________ **4.** left

_________ **5.** did

_________ **6.** won

_________ **7.** got

_________ **8.** gave

_________ **9.** met

_________ **10.** ate

_________ **11.** became

6 Practice

Complete the sentences with the simple past tense of the verbs in parentheses.

My little brother is such a brat! Two weeks ago, he (stand) ______(1)______ outside my bedroom door and (sing) ______(2)______ really loudly. It (drive) ______(3)______ me crazy. Then, he (put) ______(4)______ one of my shoes in the shower! On Monday, he (not, finish) ______(5)______ his chores, and he (not, do) ______(6)______ his homework. Last week, he (find) ______(7)______ some scissors and (cut) ______(8)______ his own hair! Last night, we (have) ______(9)______ cake for dessert, and he (eat) ______(10)______ my piece. Then, yesterday, he (take) ______(11)______ my father's keys and (drive) ______(12)______ down the block. He's ten years old!

7 Practice

Complete the story about Frida Kahlo. Write the correct form of the verbs in parentheses.

Frida Kahlo (be) ___(1)___ a famous Mexican painter. She (have) ___(2)___ a difficult life. She (catch) ___(3)___ polio at a very young age, and then a bus accident (cause) ___(4)___ her serious pain. She (live) ___(5)___ with that pain all her life. She (teach) ___(6)___ herself to paint. A mirror (hang) ___(7)___ above her bed, so she (paint) ___(8)___ many pictures of herself lying down.

In 1929, she (marry) ___(9)___ the already famous Mexican artist, Diego Rivera. In 1930, they (go) ___(10)___ to San Francisco because Diego (have) ___(11)___ a job there. In 1931, they (go) ___(12)___ to New York. In 1939, after years of traveling and many problems in their marriage, they (divorce) ___(13)___, but in 1940, they (remarry) ___(14)___. She (die) ___(15)___ in 1954. Today, her paintings are very popular and valuable.

8 Practice

Write questions and answers using the prompts.

1. Frida/have/easy life

   Did Frida have an easy life?

   No, she didn't.

2. she/catch/polio

   ______________________________?

   ______________________________.

3. car accident/cause/her pain

   ______________________________?

   ______________________________.

4. what/teach/herself

   ______________________________?

   ______________________________.

5. what/hang/above her bed

   ______________________________?

   ______________________________.

6. who/she/marry

   ______________________________?

   ______________________________.

7. when/they/go/to San Francisco

   ______________________________?

   ______________________________.

8. why/they/go/to San Francisco

   ______________________________?

   ______________________________.

9. why/they/divorce

____?

____.

10. when/she/die

____?

____.

9 Practice

Write an appropriate question for each answer.

1. **A:** What did you do last night?

   B: I watched TV and then went to bed early.

2. **A:** ____?

   B: I didn't go anywhere.

3. **A:** ____?

   B: Yes, they did.

4. **A:** ____?

   B: No, it isn't.

5. **A:** ____?

   B: To the airport.

6. **A:** ____?

   B: I went for a walk.

7. **A:** ____?

   B: At 6:00 this morning.

8. **A:** ____?

   B: My cousins.

9. **A:** ____?

   B: We had a party.

10. **A:** ____?

    B: Because she drove to work.

10 Practice

Complete the sentences using the simple past tense.

1. Yesterday, I _ate dinner_, but I didn't _eat dessert_.
2. Last summer, I ______________________, but I didn't ______________________.
3. Last night, my family didn't ______________________, but we ______________________.
4. In class today, my teacher ______________________________________,
   but he/she didn't ______________________________________.
5. Two weeks ago, my best friend ______________________________, but she/he
   didn't ______________________.

2c The Past Progressive

Student Book p. 36

11 Practice

Complete the sentences with the past progressive of the verbs in parentheses.

A. At midnight last New Year's Eve, my next-door neighbors (have) ______(1)______ a party. Some people (sing) ______(2)______ very loudly. My husband and I (watch) ______(3)______ TV, and our daughter (babysit) ______(4)______. Our young son (sleep) ______(5)______. Outside it (snow) ______(6)______, and some teenagers (light) ______(7)______ firecrackers.

B. I was very busy last summer. I (work) ______(1)______ part time and (take) ______(2)______ three classes. I (live) ______(3)______ with my parents. They (paint) ______(4)______ their house, and I (help) ______(5)______ them.

C. Driver: How fast (I, go) ______(1)______?

Police Officer: You (go) ______(2)______ 95 miles an hour!

D. Andrea: What (you, do) ______(1)______ during the power failure last week?

Justin: I (visit) ______(2)______ my brother. We (not, do) ______(3)______ anything special, but everyone in the apartment building (wonder) ______(4)______ what happened. How about you?

Andrea: I (take) ______(5)______ a shower and (wash) ______(6)______ my hair.

E. We had a terrible babysitter last Saturday. When we got home, the baby (cry) ____________ (1), and our oldest son (still, watch) ____________ (2) TV. The babysitter (talk) ____________ (3) on the phone, her boyfriend (play) ____________ (4) our children's video games, and something (burn) ____________ (5) in the kitchen!

F. Wei Lin (meet) ____________ (1) some friends for dinner last night. She (get) ____________ (2) money from the ATM. A man (look at) ____________ (3) her from across the street. A few minutes later, she (walk) ____________ (4) quickly down the street, and the man (follow) ____________ (5) her. She (get) ____________ (6) worried, so she turned around and looked at him. He (wave) ____________ (7) at her and (call) ____________ (8) her name. It was her friend Ron!

12 Practice

Write questions and answers using the prompts.

1. what/you/do/last Saturday at 9:00

   What were you doing last Saturday at 9:00?

   I wasn't doing anything special.

2. who/you/talk to/yesterday/at 2:00

   ________________________________?

   ________________________________.

3. where/you/go/yesterday morning/at 8:30

   ________________________________?

   ________________________________.

4. what/you/think about/today/in class

   ________________________________?

   ________________________________.

5. what/some of your friends/do/last night at 7:30

   ________________________________?

   ________________________________.

2d The Simple Past OR the Past Progressive

Student Book p. 40

13 Practice

Read the sentences. What does each sentence mean? Circle *a* or *b*.

1. When I got hungry, I made dinner.

a. First I got hungry, and then I made dinner.

b. I started making dinner, and then I got hungry.

2. When I got hungry, I was making dinner.

a. First I got hungry, and then I made dinner.

b. I started making dinner, and then I got hungry.

3. The children were skateboarding when it started to snow.

a. First it started to snow, and then the children skateboarded.

b. The children started skateboarding, and then it started to snow.

4. Jay called 911 when he saw the accident.

a. First he saw the accident, and then he called 911.

b. He started to call 911, and then he saw the accident.

5. My uncle was painting the house when he fell off the ladder.

a. First he fell off the ladder, and then he painted the house.

b. He started painting the house, and then he fell off the ladder.

6. When the lights went out, our husbands were playing cards.

a. First the lights went out, and then our husbands played cards.

b. Our husbands started playing cards, and then the lights went out.

7. Monique got sick while she was working at the factory.

a. First she got sick, and then she worked at the factory.

b. She started working at the factory, and then she got sick.

8. Patrick was driving home when he heard the news.

a. First he heard the news, and then he drove home.

b. He started driving before he heard the news.

9. Patrick drove home when he heard the news.

   a. First he heard the news, and then he drove home.

   b. He started driving before he heard the news.

10. Daniel danced when Mary got to the party.

   a. First Mary got to the party, and then Daniel danced.

   b. Daniel started dancing before Mary got there.

14 Practice

Complete the sentences with the correct form of the verbs in parentheses.

Galileo Galilei was born in 1564. In 1581, he (go) ________ (1) to the University of Pisa. His father (want) ________ (2) him to study medicine, but he (be) ________ (3) interested in mathematics. He (teach) ________ (4) mathematics when he (write) ________ (5) his first book, *The Little Balance.*

He (not, invent) ________ (6) the telescope, but he (improve) ________ (7) it. While he (look at) ________ (8) the sky, he (discover) ________ (9) that the moon has mountains and craters, and he (be) ________ (10) the first person to see four moons around Jupiter. He (come) ________ (11) to believe that Earth rotates around the sun, and this (make) ________ (12) him unpopular with the church.

15 Practice

Complete the sentences about you, your friends, and your family.

1. Last night while I ______________________, my roommate ______________________.
2. When I met my best friend, ____.
3. When ____, I cried.
4. ______________________________________ when my grandparents came to visit.
5. My classmates laughed when ____.
6. My father ______________________________________ when my mother met him.
7. (fill in name) ______________________________________ was talking on the phone

   when ____.
8. While ______________________________________, the teacher was talking.
9. ______________________________________ while I was sleeping last night.
10. While I was online, ____.

2e Past Time Clauses

Student Book p. 42

16 Practice

Complete the sentences.

1. Before I started this practice, ____.
2. ____ after I got home today.
3. After I got up, ____.
4. Before I was born, my parents ____.
5. While I was brushing my teeth last night, ______________________________________.
6. ____ when I got to school yesterday.
7. ____ after I went to bed.
8. Before I took this class, ____.
9. ____ when the sun rose today.
10. While I was talking to <*name*>, I ______________________________________.

2f Used To

Student Book p. 44

17 Practice

Complete the sentences using *used to* or *didn't use to* and the verbs in parentheses.

In ancient Egypt, people (write) ________________ (1) on paper like ours. Instead, they wrote on paper made from a plant that grew along the Nile River. They also (make) ________________ (2) boats, rope, and fuel from this reed and roots. This plant was called "papyrus," and the English word "paper" comes from this word. Because it was so important, the Egyptians (export) ________________ (3) it to many places in the Mediterranean. Making papyrus (be) ________________ (4) a secret, but now we know that they (cut) ________________ (5) down the reed and dry strips of the inside plant into layers. Then they (make) ________________ (6) rolls of 20 sheets each. Papyrus was so important to the ancient Egyptians, it (be) ________________ (7) a symbol of Lower Egypt.

18 Practice

Write sentences with *used to* or *didn't use to* and information from the chart.

Scott – 1988	Scott – Now
• smoked	• doesn't smoke
• lived in L.A.	• lives in Tokyo
• was a waiter	• teaches English
• was married	• is single
• didn't like rap music	• likes rap music
• didn't speak Japanese	• speaks Japanese

1. *Scott used to smoke, but now he doesn't*.
2. ____.
3. ____.
4. ____.
5. ____.
6. ____.

SELF-TEST

A Choose the best answer, A, B, C, or D, to complete the sentence. Mark your answer by darkening the oval with the same letter.

1. Glen and Jill ________ in Hong Kong when they broke up.

A. were stay (A) (B) (C) (D)
B. were staying
C. was staying
D. stayed

2. Han Jong ________ smoke.

A. use to (A) (B) (C) (D)
B. was
C. used to
D. were

3. I ________ dinner before I called you.

A. ate (A) (B) (C) (D)
B. eat
C. eated
D. was eat

4. While the ship ________, the band was playing.

A. sank (A) (B) (C) (D)
B. sinked
C. sink
D. was sinking

5. What ________ you do last summer?

A. used to (A) (B) (C) (D)
B. did
C. were
D. do

6. When ________ you using the computer?

A. did (A) (B) (C) (D)
B. was
C. do
D. were

7. Who was ________ the music so loudly?

A. playing (A) (B) (C) (D)
B. play
C. played
D. used to play

8. They ________ the accident when they looked out the window.

A. were seeing (A) (B) (C) (D)
B. saw
C. see
D. used to saw

9. When Professor Wilkinson was teaching at the university, what ________ he discover?

A. do (A) (B) (C) (D)
B. did
C. was
D. were

10. I ________ you!

A. heard (A) (B) (C) (D)
B. was hearing
C. hearing
D. were hearing

B Find the underlined word or phrase, A, B, C, or D, that is incorrect. Mark your answer by darkening the oval with the same letter.

1. The Garcias were have (A) dinner in their backyard when (B) it (C) started (D) to rain.

   (A) (B) (C) (D)

2. Yoon was (A) crossing (B) the street when (C) I sawed (D) him.

   (A) (B) (C) (D)

3. While (A) Isabelle was (B) taking (C) a shower, she fall (D).

   (A) (B) (C) (D)

4. The president were (A) visiting his parents when (B) he (C) heard (D) the news.

   (A) (B) (C) (D)

5. Girls (A) didn't use (B) to be allowed to wearing (C) pants at school (D).

   (A) (B) (C) (D)

6. The train (A) was approach (B) the station when (C) Mr. Hendrix got (D) there.

   (A) (B) (C) (D)

7. Alexander likes (A) soccer now (B), but he didn't (C) used to (D).

   (A) (B) (C) (D)

8. Before (A) she became (B) famous, she use to (C) drive (D) taxis in New York City.

   (A) (B) (C) (D)

9. While (A) she (B) opened the refrigerator, the butter (C) dropped (D) out.

   (A) (B) (C) (D)

10. While (A) Rick was (B) working (C), he haved (D) a great idea.

    (A) (B) (C) (D)

UNIT 3 THE FUTURE

3a *Be Going To*

Student Book p. 52

1 Practice

Read the sentences. Write *F* next to the sentence if it is in the future. Write *N* if the sentence is happening now (the present).

__N__ **1.** Carrie's shopping for vegetables.

_____ **2.** She's going to buy some groceries.

_____ **3.** Ing Chul isn't doing her homework right now.

_____ **4.** She's going to stay after school.

_____ **5.** Ellen and Young are walking to the cafeteria.

_____ **6.** They're going to eat dinner.

_____ **7.** Michi isn't going to go to college next year.

_____ **8.** He's going to work for a plant farm.

_____ **9.** I'm not going to the post office now.

_____ **10.** I'm going to go there later.

2 Practice

What is going to happen? Complete the sentences with *be going to.*

A. Jackie is reading a book on the couch. Her little brother is sneaking up behind her very quietly. He has a whistle in his hand and a big smile on his face. She doesn't hear him. What is going to happen?

1. Jackie is going to __be angry____________________.

2. She isn't going to ________________________.

3. Her little brother is going to ____________________.

4. He isn't going to ________________________.

B. Hiro has his passport and is waiting at the airport. He's happy, but he's also a little nervous.

1. Hiro ______________________________.

2. He (not) ______________________________.

C. Ira is really tired, but he's making cookies now. He falls asleep, and the cookies are still in the oven.

1. The cookies ______________________________.

2. The cookies (not) ______________________________.

3. Ira ______________________________.

4. Ira (not) ______________________________.

D. Today is Sammy's birthday. His friends are hiding in his living room. They have presents and a cake for him. He doesn't know they're there.

1. Sammy ______________________________.

2. His friends ______________________________.

3. Sammy (not) ______________________________.

4. His friends (not) ______________________________.

E. Ted and Janine are engaged to be married next month. Janine isn't happy about this. She wants to wait a little while longer. She asks Ted to meet her for dinner at their favorite restaurant.

1. Janine ______________________________.

2. She (not) ______________________________.

3. Ted ______________________________.

4. He (not) ______________________________.

3 Practice

Read Lisa's to-do list. Write questions and answers using an appropriate verb and *be going to*.

1. *Is she going to do her laundry?*

   Yes, she is.

2. ______________________________?

   ______________________________.

3. ______________________________?

   ______________________________.

4. ______________________________?

   ______________________________.

5. ______________________________?

   ______________________________.

6. ______________________________?

   ______________________________.

7. ______________________________?

   ______________________________.

8. ______________________________?

   ______________________________.

4 Practice

Write questions and answers about you in the future using *be going to* and the prompts.

1. do laundry

   Are you going to do laundry?

   Yes, I am. (OR) *No, I'm not.*

2. learn to cook Indian food

   ______________________________?

   ______________________________.

3. teach English

____?

____.

4. paint your apartment

____?

____.

5. go snowboarding

____?

____.

6. use a digital camera

____?

____.

7. play in a band

____?

____.

3b *Will*

Student Book p. 55

5 Practice

Complete the sentences with *will* and the verbs in parentheses. You may use contractions or full forms.

1. Mary: Who's going to pick up Dave?

   Stacey: I'm not doing anything. I (do) *'ll do / will do* it.

2. Will: Tomorrow is my first day of teaching. I'm really nervous.

   Rosemary: Don't worry. You (be) ______________ fine.

3. Grandfather to granddaughter:

You're going to visit New York with your dad. You're going to see so many things! You (see) ________________ skyscrapers. You (eat) ________________ many different foods. You (ride) ________________ the subway, and you (have) ________________ a wonderful time.

4. Mom: Jeff, when are you going to do your homework?

Jeff: I (do) ________________ it after dinner.

5. Oh, man. The bus is late. I (not, have) ________________ time for coffee.

6. Abeer: I'm leaving now.

Jasmine: Okay. I (see) ________________ you tomorrow.

7. Mary Jo: Amy, there's someone at the door.

Amy: Okay, I (be) ________________ right there.

8. Stan: What smells so good? I'm hungry!

Ivanna: Lasagna. I (get) ________________ you some.

9. No! I already told you. I (not, do) ________________ it!

10. I'm going to buy a computer, and I predict that my life (change) ________________. I think that I (do) ________________ everything online. I (order) ________________ food online, and the grocer (deliver) ________________ the groceries. I (reserve) ________________ DVDs and (make) ________________ reservations for restaurants online. I (not, buy) ________________ plane or train tickets from the travel agent. I (not, pay) ________________ bills by mail either. Life (be) ________________ much easier!

11. Cindy: What does your horoscope say?

Terri: It says that I (have) ________________ a good week. I (not, have) ________________ a lot of money, but a lot of friends (call) ________________ me.

3c *Be Going To* OR *Will*

Student Book p. 59

6 Practice

Write *will* or *be going to* beside each future situation.

1. a plan you made before now ______________
2. a prediction for the future ______________
3. a future event that is the result of a present situation ______________
4. a plan you make right now ______________

Write an example of each future situation. Use *will* or *be going to*.

Example: Karen's going to Paris for her summer vacation.

1. ______________________________.
2. ______________________________.
3. ______________________________.
4. ______________________________.

7 Practice

Complete the sentences with *will* or *be going to* and the verbs in parentheses.

A. Jeremy: I'm having a party on Saturday. I'm asking everyone to bring something.

Liz: Okay. I (bring) ______________ (1) potato salad.

Kurt: I (make) ______________ (2) a cake.

Steve: I (get) ______________ (3) the drinks.

Jeremy: Great. It (be) ______________ (4) fun. I (see) ______________ (5) you there!

B. Jill: We (go) ____________ camping this weekend.
(1)

Tim: That sounds like fun.

Jill: Yeah. We (leave) ____________ Friday night.
(2)

Tim: Where (go, you) ____________?
(3)

Jill: We're not sure yet, but we (probably, camp) ____________ somewhere near the coast.
(4)

C. Dolores: I think I (call) ____________ the massage therapist to make an appointment this week.
(1)

Lupe: Why? What's wrong?

Dolores: Nothing. I (run) ____________ the marathon in November, so I'm training now and sometimes I'm sore after a long run.
(2)

Lupe: That's great. Good luck!

D. Penny: I don't have time to talk right now. I (talk) ____________ to you tonight. I hope to be home early.

Marci: Okay.

E. Annie: Are you busy? I (meet) ____________ some people at the coffee shop. Want to come with me?
(1)

Ted: Sure. I (go) ____________ with you.
(2)

F. Mikey: I (be) ____________ an artist when I grow up.
(1)

Courtney: I (be) ____________ a doctor.
(2)

Luke: I (be) ____________ an Olympic ski jumper.
(3)

3d The Present Progressive to Express Future Time

Student Book p. 60

8 Practice

Read the sentences. Write *F* next to the sentence if it is in the future. Write *N* if the sentence is happening now (the present).

_____ **1.** I'm getting a new computer and returning this one tomorrow.

_____ **2.** I'm taking some time off from work next week.

_____ **3.** Dad's taking a shower.

_____ **4.** He's singing in the shower.

_____ **5.** We aren't getting cable TV when we move into the new house.

_____ **6.** We're packing now.

_____ **7.** My tomatoes aren't doing well.

_____ **8.** They're not getting enough sun.

_____ **9.** I'm planting lettuce tomorrow.

_____ **10.** What are you doing?

_____ **11.** What are you doing tonight?

9 Practice

Complete the sentences using the present progressive to express the future of the verbs in parentheses.

A. Denise: We (have) ______________ (1) a bonfire tonight.

Rick: Who (come) ______________ (2)?

Denise: Sally, Devon, Maria, Christopher, and Vince.

Rick: What (bring) ______________ (3) everyone ______________ (3)?

Denise: Well, Vince (bring) ______________ (4) corn to cook over the fire.

B. Hillary: When (leave) ______________ you ______________ tomorrow?

Phil: At 9:00.

C. Simon: What (do) ______________ (1) you ______________ (1) this weekend?

Bill: I (have) ______________ (2) my boss over for dinner on Saturday, but on Sunday, I (not, do) ______________ (3) anything.

D. Kyle (enter) ________ (1) college in the fall. He (work) ________ (2) at a summer camp to save money before then. He's a little sad because his girlfriend (attend) ________ (3) a different school.

10 Practice

Jessica Raymond is a famous mystery writer. Read her schedule for tomorrow.

7:00	go over schedule with Jonathon
8:00	work out with trainer
9:00	light breakfast with publicist
10:30–12:00	meeting with accountant
12:00	lunch with editor
2:00–4:00	work
4:30–6:00	book signing
7:00	dinner with family
8:00–11:30	relax at home

She's talking with her assistant Jonathon about her schedule. Complete the sentences with the present progressive to express the future.

Jessica: What (do) ________ (1) I ________ (1) tomorrow?

Jonathon: Well, at 7:00, you ________ (2).

Jessica: And after that?

Jonathon: You ________ (3) at 8:00, and at 9:00, you ________ (4).

Jessica: (meet) ________ (5) I ________ (5) with my accountant?

Jonathon: Yes, from 10:30 to 12:00.

Jessica: Who (have) ________ (6) I ________ (6) lunch with?

Jonathon: Your editor. Then you ________ (7) from 2:00 to 4:00.

Jessica: When (do) ________ (8) I ________ (8) the book signing?

Jonathon: From 4:30 to 6:00.

3e The Simple Present to Express Future Time

Student Book p. 62

11 Practice

Look at the cruise ship's itinerary. Then complete the sentences with the verbs in parentheses using the simple present tense to express the future.

Date	Destination	Time
February 6	Miami	5:00 PM
February 7	day at sea	
February 8	Jamaica	7:00 AM – 6:00 PM
February 9	Grand Cayman	9:00 AM – 7:00 PM
February 10	Mexico	8:00 AM – 8:00 PM
February 11	day at sea	
February 12	Miami	11:00 AM

The trip includes a bike tour on Grand Cayman and a shopping trip in Jamaica. Scuba diving lessons are available in Mexico.

Dale: Tell me about your trip. When (leave) ______ (1) you ______ (1)?

Kiomi: We (leave) ______ (2) from Miami on February 6th. We (have) ______ (3) a day at sea, and then we (arrive) ______ (4) in Jamaica on February 8th.

Dale: What (be) ______ (5) your plans there?

Kiomi: We (shop) ______ (6) and (go) ______ (7) sightseeing. The ship (depart) ______ (8) Jamaica at 6:00 PM, and it (arrive) ______ (9) in Grand Cayman the next day. There, we (take) ______ (10) a bike trip. On February 10th, we (have) ______ (11) a day in Mexico, and we (learn) ______ (12) how to scuba dive. Then the ship (have) ______ (13) one last day at sea, and we (return) ______ (14) to Miami on the 12th.

Dale: Sounds like fun!

12 Practice

Think about your plans this weekend. Write them using *be going to,* the present progressive, or the simple present tense.

1. a. I'm going to go to a party.
   b. I'm going to a party.
   c. At 7:00 on Saturday, I go to a party.
2. a. ____________________.
   b. ____________________.
   c. ____________________.
3. a. ____________________.
   b. ____________________.
   c. ____________________.

3f The Future Conditional

Student Book p. 63

13 Practice

Read the following sentences. Circle the condition and underline the result.

1. Sylvie will make cookies if she has any chocolate chips.
2. She'll bring them to the party if she has enough.
3. If she brings enough cookies, everyone will be happy.
4. If there aren't enough cookies, some people will be disappointed.
5. She'll make more cookies if people ask her.

14 Practice

Complete the sentences using the simple present tense or *will* and the verbs in parentheses.

1. If I (make) ____________ a lot of money, I (get) ____________ a big house and car.
2. I (have) ____________ a lot of parties if (live) ____________ in a big house.
3. I (be) ____________ popular if I (have) ____________ a lot of parties.

4. If I (be) ______________ popular, I (have) ______________ a lot of influence.
5. I (take) ______________ on more responsibilities if I (have) ______________ a lot of influence.
6. If I (have) ______________ more responsibilities, I (be) ______________ very busy.
7. I (not, be) ______________ happy if I (be) ______________ too busy.
8. If I (not, be) ______________ happy, I (get) ______________ depressed.

15 Practice

Complete the sentences using the simple present tense or *will* and an appropriate verb.

1. If I'm successful, ____.
2. ____ if I don't finish school.
3. If the world stays the same, ____.
4. ____ if violence doesn't stop.
5. If ____, people will live longer.
6. If I speak English fluently, ____.
7. If ________________________________, I won't make the same mistakes.
8. Air pollution will decrease if ____.
9. If I stop watching TV, ____.
10. If ____, I'll exercise more.

3g Future Time Clauses

Student Book p. 65

16 Practice

Write *C* next to the sentence if the result and condition are correct. Write *I* if the result and condition are incorrect.

_____ 1. When Dale will pick up his son, they'll go to the grocery store.

_____ 2. As soon as Doug gets home, he walk his dog.

_____ 3. Rose will take a nap after she eats lunch.

_____ 4. You'll want to put the ice cream in the freezer when you get home.

_____ 5. Everyone will present his/her work before we leave today.

______ 6. When you know the assignment, will you call me?

______ 7. Hae Jung will be in Paris after she's in Rome.

______ 8. If we will find a babysitter, we'll attend the concert.

______ 9. The Lees will leave as soon as the wedding will be over.

______ 10. If you eat that, you won't sleep well.

17 Practice

Complete the sentences using information from the recipe.

How to Make a Vanilla Milkshake

1. Put two scoops of good vanilla ice cream in a blender.
2. Fill the blender almost to the top with milk.
3. Turn on the blender and blend slowly.
4. Pour the milkshake into a large glass and enjoy.
5. You can add chocolate syrup, fruit, and nuts if you like.

1. Before ___*you add the milk*___, put the ice cream in the blender.
2. ________________________ after you turn on the blender.
3. Before you pour the milkshake into a glass, ________________________.
4. ________________________ after you pour the milkshake into a glass.

18 Practice

Describe a process using the prompts.

How to ______________________________

1. Before ______________________________,
______________________________.
2. ______________________________ as soon as
______________________________.
3. ______________________________ after
______________________________.
4. When ______________________________,
______________________________.

19 Practice

Complete the sentences.

1. When I finish this exercise, ______________________________.
2. ______________________________ before I go to school tomorrow.
3. When I have enough money, ______________________________.
4. ______________________________ as soon as I
______________________________.
5. ______________________________ after
______________________________.

SELF-TEST

A Choose the best answer, A, B, C, or D, to complete the sentence. Mark your answer by darkening the oval with the same letter.

1. _______ people don't recycle, there'll be more problems in the environment.

A. After
B. If
C. Before
D. When

Ⓐ Ⓑ Ⓒ Ⓓ

2. Sarah's plane _______ at noon.

A. departs
B. will departs
C. going to depart
D. is depart

Ⓐ Ⓑ Ⓒ Ⓓ

3. If Max shaves his head, his girlfriend _______ furious!

A. will
B. is
C. going to be
D. will be

Ⓐ Ⓑ Ⓒ Ⓓ

4. Jason will study history _______ he doesn't get into law school.

A. after
B. if
C. before
D. when

Ⓐ Ⓑ Ⓒ Ⓓ

5. He'll feel better if he _______.

A. is going to exercise
B. will exercise
C. exercises
D. is exercise

Ⓐ Ⓑ Ⓒ Ⓓ

6. Tommy and Ashley _______ married next week.

A. get
B. will get
C. are getting
D. going to get

Ⓐ Ⓑ Ⓒ Ⓓ

7. As soon as Julie _______ her children, she'll kiss them.

A. will see
B. is seeing
C. is going to
D. sees

Ⓐ Ⓑ Ⓒ Ⓓ

8. Who _______ with us to the beach on Saturday?

A. is coming
B. will come
C. comes
D. going to come

Ⓐ Ⓑ Ⓒ Ⓓ

9. Dr. Learner _______ to his staff after his last patient tomorrow.

A. talks
B. will talks
C. is going to
D. is talking

Ⓐ Ⓑ Ⓒ Ⓓ

10. After Candace _______ the picture, they'll take a break.

A. is hanging
B. will hang
C. hangs
D. is going to hang

Ⓐ Ⓑ Ⓒ Ⓓ

B Find the underlined word or phrase, A, B, C, or D, that is incorrect. Mark your answer by darkening the oval with the same letter.

1. Myra and Steve going (A) to the hardware store. They (B) intend (C) to repair (D) their front door.

   (A) (B) (C) (D)

2. Roberto meets (A) us (B) at the theater in (C) two hours (D).

   (A) (B) (C) (D)

3. The Clarks leave (A) tomorrow at 8:00 because their plane is depart (B) at 9:30. They don't (C) want (D) to be late.

   (A) (B) (C) (D)

4. After (A) Nancy will send (B) email, she'll (C) fax (D) the brochure.

   (A) (B) (C) (D)

5. By the year 2020, people (A) aren't use (B) cars anymore. They'll (C) ride (D) small scooters.

   (A) (B) (C) (D)

6. Charlotte won't (A) time to see (B) you this morning (C). She's (D) already late.

   (A) (B) (C) (D)

7. In the future, children study (A) at home because schools (B) won't (C) exist (D).

   (A) (B) (C) (D)

8. If (A) Vern finishes (B) the repairs, he (C) starts work (D) in the yard.

   (A) (B) (C) (D)

9. You going (A) to love (B) my brother (C). He's (D) hilarious!

   (A) (B) (C) (D)

10. Melissa returns (A) at 10:00. She's (B) going to be (C) at the hotel later. We see (D) her then.

    (A) (B) (C) (D)

UNIT 4 NOUNS, ARTICLES, AND QUANTITY

4a Singular and Plural Nouns

Student Book p. 74

1 Practice

Write *C* next to the word if the singular or plural is correct. Write *I* if the singular or plural is incorrect.

__I__ **1.** leafs

_____ **2.** photos

_____ **3.** a children

_____ **4.** tomatoes

_____ **5.** glasses

_____ **6.** a orange

_____ **7.** a men

_____ **8.** a tornado

_____ **9.** a woman

_____ **10.** countries

_____ **11.** an echo

_____ **12.** a foot

_____ **13.** parties

_____ **14.** a animal

_____ **15.** an mouse

2 Practice

Lydia and Susan have just moved into a new apartment. Complete the sentences with the correct plural of the word in parentheses.

Lydia: Where are the (dish) ____________ (1)?

Susan: They're in those (box) ____________ (2).

Lydia: Okay. I'm putting the (knife) ____________ (3) in the drawer over here.

Susan: I'll put the (glass) ____________ (4) on the shelf.

Lydia: We need new (pot) ____________ (5) and (pan) ____________ (6). These are too old.

Susan: And we need clean (sponge) ____________ (7) for the kitchen. I'll make a shopping list.

Lydia: Okay. I'll go to the store. I'm hungry. Are you?

Susan: Yes.

Lydia: I'll pick up some (sandwich) ____________ (8) and (soda) ____________ (9).

3 Practice

Sara is a meteorologist. Read her weather report and complete the sentences with the correct plural of the word in parentheses.

There was some unusual weather around the world this past week. In Martinique, two (volcano) ___(1)___ erupted at the same time. People left their (home) ___(2)___ in (bus) ___(3)___.

Closer to home, a series of (tornado) ___(4)___ raced across much of the country. They sent (man) ___(5)___, (woman) ___(6)___, and (child) ___(7)___ to basements for safety. The wind blew down several (house) ___(8)___, and many homes lost (roof) ___(9)___.

4 Practice

Complete the sentences with the correct plural of the words in parentheses.

Blaine enjoys living in the country. He can sit on his porch with his dog and look out at the (cow) ___(1)___ and (sheep) ___(2)___ in the field. His (chicken) ___(3)___ are running around the yard, and (horse) ___(4)___ are in the barn. His (cat) ___(5)___ are in the house. (Wolf) ___(6)___ and (mouse) ___(7)___ roam through the woods.

4b Nouns as Subjects, Objects, and Objects of Prepositions

Student Book p. 78

5 Practice

Read the sentence. Then read each statement about the sentence and write *C* next to the statement if it is correct. Write *I* if it is incorrect.

The children are riding the Ferris wheel at the fair.

_____ **1.** *The Ferris wheel* is the subject.

_____ **2.** *At* is a preposition.

_____ **3.** *The children* is the object.

_____ **4.** *The fair* is the object of the preposition.

6 Practice

Label the subject (S), verb (V), object (O), preposition (P), and the object of the preposition (OP) in the following sentences.

1. Some children are playing games near the Ferris wheel.

2. Some people are eating cotton candy on a stick.

3. We're watching acrobats on a tightrope.

4. Francie won a giant toy airplane for her daughter.

5. I'm making lunch for the kids.

6. I put the sandwiches on the table.

7. The children are taking a nap after lunch.

7 Practice

Write sentences, putting the words in the correct order. Then label the sentence parts as in Practice 6. Pay special attention to questions.

1. the onions/the sink/Carol/at/cut

Carol cut the onions at the sink ________.
S V O P OP

2. put/she/the oven/the lasagna/in

____.

3. dinner/after/we/the dishes/do/wash

____?

4. us/called/the bank/from/David

____.

5. are buying/the corner market/at/you/vegetables

____?

6. his veterinarian/from/is eating/Sammy/special food

____?

7. bought/from/he/my brother/a set of knives

____.

8. to/her parents/them/the beach/took

____.

9. the guests/the party/did/follow/to/the directions

____?

10. Monday/I/on/have/a dentist's appointment

____.

11. in/a label/does/need/the package/its corner

____?

12. the clock/on/hung/the wall/ they

____.

4c Count Nouns and Noncount Nouns

Student Book p. 80

8 Practice

Write *C* if the noun is a count noun. Write *N* if the noun is a noncount noun.

_____ **1.** fork
_____ **2.** weather
_____ **3.** clouds
_____ **4.** rain
_____ **5.** tornadoes
_____ **6.** food
_____ **7.** cheese
_____ **8.** milk
_____ **9.** bottles
_____ **10.** cards
_____ **11.** information
_____ **12.** smoke
_____ **13.** cigarettes
_____ **14.** money
_____ **15.** dollars
_____ **16.** mail
_____ **17.** letters
_____ **18.** email
_____ **19.** exercises
_____ **20.** homework

9 Practice

Complete the conversations with the correct form of the nouns in parentheses. Use the singular form for noncount nouns. Use the plural form for count nouns.

A. At a bank, Mr. Hopkins is applying for a loan.

I have two (child) ______(1)______, and I'm helping to pay for their (education) ______(2)______. They both go to good (university) ______(3)______. They both have (job) ______(4)______, but they don't make enough (money) ______(5)______ to pay for all of their (expense) ______(6)______. Their (happiness) ______(7)______ is very important to me.

B. Lily: What did you have for lunch?

Tom: I had (soup) ______(1)______ and (cracker) ______(2)______. For dessert, I had (fruit) ______(3)______ and (cookie) ______(4)______.

C. Ms. Cone: Why did you move to Florida?

Mr. Jeter: I hated the (weather) ______________ (1) back home. I was sick of (snow) ______________ (2), (wind) ______________ (3), and (ice) ______________ (4). Here there's no (smog) ______________ (5) or (pollution) ______________ (6), just good clean (air) ______________ (7), (sunshine) ______________ (8), (sand) ______________ (9), and (water) ______________ (10).

D. A stylist to a customer at a hair salon:

Stylist: Your hair is really dry! How do you take care of it?

Customer: I wash it with (soap) ______________ (1).

Stylist: You need to use (shampoo) ______________ (2) and (conditioner) ______________ (3). I'll treat it today with hot (oil) ______________ (4).

E. Brad: What's your favorite subject?

Scott: I like (history) ______________ (1). What about you?

Brad: I like (biology) ______________ (2), but I'm interested in a lot of (subject) ______________ (3).

F. This is fat-free (ice cream) ______________ (1). We'll lose (weight) ______________ (2) without the (guilt) ______________ (3) about eating a lot of it.

G. Two roommates to a police officer:

Elizabeth: They took my (jewelry) ______________ (1), (money) ______________ (2), and good (luggage) ______________ (3).

Police Officer: Anything else?

Jane: I think that's it. They left the two (television) ______________ (1) and the two (laptop) ______________ (2), but they destroyed my expensive (rug) ______________ (3) and (furniture) ______________ (4).

H. Diplomat's speech at a special party:

We are experiencing (peace) ________(1) for the first time in many years, and there is much (progress) ________(2) in (technology) ________(3). We are now the world leader in producing (steel) ________(4), so there are many (job) ________(5) and a lot of (work) ________(6) for our people. We don't have much (poverty) ________(7), and the general (health) ________(8) of all citizens is getting better and better.

10 Practice

Write as many nouns as you can for the following categories.

Things in your room

laptop

CDs

____

____

____

____

Things you want in your future

____

____

____

____

Things in your kitchen

____

____

____

____

4d *A, An,* and *Some*

Student Book p. 83

11 Practice

Write *C* next to the phrase if *a, an,* or *some* is correct. Write *I* if *a, an,* or *some* is incorrect.

_____ **1.** a money

_____ **2.** a dollar

_____ **3.** some gasoline

_____ **4.** an eggs

_____ **5.** an advice

_____ **6.** some knowledge

_____ **7.** a games

_____ **8.** some fun

_____ **9.** an exercise

_____ **10.** a homework

_____ **11.** a mail

_____ **12.** some ice cream

_____ **13.** some work

_____ **14.** a class

12 Practice

Write sentences, putting the words in the correct order.

1. a/food/some/they/in/put/basket

They put some food in a basket.

2. for/Kerry/furniture/apartment/some/bought/an

____.

3. an/mail/envelope/in/I/the/put/

____.

4. iron/there/steel/an/is/some/and/automobile/in

____.

5. cold/he/he/and/some/a/has/needs/medicine

____.

13 Practice

Complete the sentences with *a, an,* or *some*.

A. Ann: I'm going to sell my car, and I need to clean it out.

Bob: What's in it?

Ann: In the trunk, there's ______ (1) oil, ______ (2) water, ______ (3) spare tire, and ______ (4) flashlight. In the front, there's ______ (5) map, ______ (6) gum, ______ (7) paper, and ______ (8) pen.

B. Maria: What are you taking on your trip?

Domingo: I'm taking ______ (1) suitcase, ______ (2) clothes, ______ (3) umbrella, ______ (4) jacket, ______ (5) watch, and ______ (6) cologne.

C. Laurie: Wow. There's nothing to eat in your refrigerator.

Kathy: I know. I need to go shopping. Let's see... there's ______ (1) brown lettuce, ______ (2) egg, ______ (3) old frozen pizza, ______ (4) ice cream, ______ (5) tofu, and ______ (6) old orange. Yuck. Let's go out.

4e *Some, Any, Much, Many, A Little, A Few,* and *A Lot Of*

Student Book p. 84

14 Practice

Complete the conversations with *some, any, much, many, a little, a few,* or *a lot of*. More than one answer may be possible.

A. Margaret is talking to her friend Suzanne about her new house.

Margaret: I love the place! There are ______ (1) nice neighbors, and there isn't ______ (2) traffic.

Suzanne: Are there ______ (3) parks?

Margaret: Yes. And there isn't ______ (4) crime or noise. There are ______ (5) restaurants and ______ (6) markets.

B. Dennis: How was your vacation?

Rod: We didn't have ________ (1) fun. There was ________ (2) rain, and there wasn't ________ (3) sun.

C. Keith is a car salesman, and he's getting his yearly job performance review. He is not having a good year.

Boss: Keith, you're not having ________ (1) luck this year.

Keith: I know.

Boss: You have ________ (2) knowledge and ________ (3) experience.

Are you having ________ (4) other problems?

Keith: No, not really.

Boss: Do you need ________ (5) time off? Do you need ________ (6) help?

Keith: No, thanks. Business will get better.

15 Practice

Read the facts about Rapa Nui. Write sentences using the information, the words, and *some, any, much, many, a little, a few,* or *a lot of.*

Facts about Rapa Nui (Easter Island)

Population:	3000
Size:	160 square km
Industry:	tourism and wool export (15,000 tourists/year)
Jobs:	farming, raising sheep for wool
National affiliation:	Chile
Government:	citizens do not pay taxes
Languages:	Spanish and Rapanui
Moais (head statues):	600
Height of Moais:	3-12 m (10-14 ft.)
Weight of Moais:	some Moais are over 50 tons

jobs land Moais people tourism tourists wool

1. *There is a lot of / some tourism on Rapa Nui.*
2. ______________________________.
3. ______________________________.
4. ______________________________.
5. ______________________________.
6. ______________________________.
7. ______________________________.

4f *Few, A Few, Little,* and *A Little*

Student Book p. 86

16 Practice

Write *C* next to the phrase if *few, a few, little,* or *a little* is used correctly. Write *I* if *few, a few, little,* or *a little* is used incorrectly.

_____	**1.** a little clothing	_____	**6.** little weight
_____	**2.** a few shoes	_____	**7.** a few advice
_____	**3.** few homework	_____	**8.** a little information
_____	**4.** a little questions	_____	**9.** a little ideas
_____	**5.** few people	_____	**10.** a few beauty

17 Practice

Complete the sentences with *a few, few, a little,* or *little.*

1. I'm thirsty. I need __________ water.
2. It rained a lot last week. The garden needs __________ water.
3. Nadine: Are you hungry?
   Karl: __________. I only had some toast earlier today.
4. Office worker: I need __________ help. My printer isn't printing.
   Computer technician: We're having __________ problems with the network today.
5. Daphne: No one came to the party.
   Murray: __________ people knew about it.

6. Hyung: Do you want to come with me?

   Jae: Sure. I need ________________ minutes to get ready.

   Hyung: That's okay. I need ________________ time, too.

7. This room is very dull. It needs ________________ color.

8. Their son doesn't like school. There are ________________ subjects he enjoys.

9. It was very hot last night. I got ________________ sleep, so I'm really tired today.

10. Doctor: Does it hurt?

    Patient: Not really. There's ________________ pain.

11. Eat ________________ vegetables, but ________________ butter and sugar.

12. We're going to be in Hawaii, so don't take a lot. You need ________________ clothing—just a swimsuit, shorts, and t-shirts.

13. Adam: How's business?

    Tom: Pretty good. I have ________________ clients now.

14. They canceled the class. ________________ students came.

15. I'm finishing my homework. I have ________________ pages to read.

16. Let's go for a walk. I need ________________ exercise.

17. Andrew isn't very popular. He has ________________ friends. I think he's lonely.

4g Units of Measure with Nouns

Student Book p. 88

18 Practice

Write *C* next to the phrase if the quantity with the noncount noun is correct. Write *I* if the quantity with the noncount noun is incorrect.

_____ 1. a tube of information

_____ 2. a slice of chips

_____ 3. a can of soup

_____ 4. a carton of jam

_____ 5. a can of lettuce

_____ 6. a head of toilet paper

_____ 7. three cups of sugar

_____ 8. a piece of water

_____ 9. a bottle of water

_____ 10. a bar of soap

19 Practice

You're going to make dinner for friends. You're serving salad, spaghetti, garlic bread, and fruit. Complete the shopping list with units of measure. More than one answer may be correct.

1. ____________ spaghetti
2. ____________ tomatoes
3. ____________ lettuce
4. ____________ tomato sauce
5. ____________ cheese
6. ____________ carrots
7. ____________ bread
8. ____________ garlic
9. ____________ grapes
10. ____________ oranges

4h Possessive Nouns

Student Book p. 90

20 Practice

Read the following possessive phrases. If the possessive is plural, write *P* next to the phrase. If the possessive is singular, write *S*.

_____ 1. the woman's shoes

_____ 2. the women's shoes

_____ 3. my son's soccer game

_____ 4. my daughters' skates

_____ 5. the students' complaints

_____ 6. the artist's paintings

_____ 7. the artists' paintings

_____ 8. the children's room

_____ 9. the child's room

_____ 10. my parents' TV

21 Practice

Add apostrophes in the correct place to the underlined nouns to show possession.

This is our childrens (1) school. These are the students (2) desks, this is the teachers (3) lounge, and here are the schools (4) computers. Oh, there's a childs (5) jacket on the floor. There are eight levels in the school. The upper levels (6) rooms are over here, and the lower levels (7) rooms are down the hall.

But there is a problem. The schools (8) roof is leaking, and the students (9) textbooks are old. We need to change a few things here. Our childrens (10) education is very important.

22 Practice

Rewrite the sentences to show possession.

1. These are the fashions of this year.

These are this year's fashions ______.

2. I disagree with the opinions of the newspapers.

______.

3. Did you see the new menus of the two restaurants last week?

______?

4. We studied the movies of Alfred Hitchcock.

______.

5. Those are the designs of Nancy.

______.

6. I don't know the name of my teacher.

______.

7. Today is the birthday of my twin sisters.

______.

8. Oh, there's the cat of my neighbor.

______.

4i *A, An,* or *The*

Student Book p. 92

23 Practice

Complete the sentences with *the, a,* or *an.*

A. It is Roberta's birthday. Her best friend, Chloe, bought ________ (1) ring for her. Chloe and Roberta went to ________ (2) restaurant. ________ (3) restaurant was near Chloe's house. In ________ (4) restaurant, she gave ________ (5) ring to her friend.

B. Baseball is ________ (1) popular sport. There is ________ (2) baseball field in our park. A lot of people meet in ________ (3) park every weekend. There's going to be ________ (4) baseball game today. We're going to ________ (5) game in an hour.

C. Here's how to make ________ (1) omelet. You'll need three eggs, ________ (2) quarter cup of cream, and some salt and pepper. Break ________ (3) eggs into ________ (4) bowl. Mix them well, and add ________ (5) cream and salt and pepper. Put some oil in ________ (6) small frying pan on the stove. When ________ (7) pan is hot, put ________ (8) egg mixture in it. Cook it.

D. Luis takes his car to ________ (1) garage on Division Street. ________ (2) people there are great. Last summer, he needed ________ (3) new tire. They gave him ________ (4) tire at a really good price.

E. Raymond has ________ (1) new cell phone and ________ (2) new number. ________ (3) phone is very small and ________ (4) number is easy to remember.

F. I had ________ (1) really bad day yesterday. I got in ________ (2) car accident and was late to work. Then I bought ________ (3) cup of coffee. I put ________ (4) cup on my desk, and then I hit it with my hand. ________ (5) cup fell, and ________ (6) coffee got on my clothes and shoes. I was happy when ________ (7) day was over.

G. Janine: What did you get?

Frank: I got some apples, ____________ (1) loaf of bread, ____________ (2) bottle of milk, ____________ (3) orange, and ____________ (4) bag of chips.

Janine: Great. Please put ____________ (5) apples and ____________ (6) orange on the counter. ____________ (7) milk goes in the refrigerator, and ____________ (8) loaf of bread goes in the freezer. I'll take ____________ (9) chips.

H. Kyle: What did you get for graduation?

Alex: I got ____________ (1) new laptop, some money, and some new shoes. I'm taking ____________ (2) laptop with me to the dorm next year. I put ____________ (3) money in the bank, and I'm wearing ____________ (4) new shoes.

I. Claudine: Have you seen Jose's new house?

Paula: Yes. It's really big. There are two bathrooms. ____________ (1) one upstairs is very big and light. ____________ (2) one downstairs is smaller. ____________ (3) kitchen is very modern, and ____________ (4) living room connects ____________ (5) family room to ____________ (6) dining room. ____________ (7) front yard is nice, too.

J. Scott: That was ____________ (1) interesting presentation.

Elaine: Thank you. Do you think ____________ (2) graphics were too complicated?

Scott: No. They were fine.

Elaine: Did you understand ____________ (3) statistics?

Scott: Yes. And I think ____________ (4) charts were very clear. You're going to be ____________ (5) excellent chairperson of our group.

4j Generalizations

Student Book p. 94

24 Practice

Write *C* next to the sentence if *the* is used correctly. Write *I* if *the* is used incorrectly.

__I__ **1.** The computers are very useful.

__C__ **2.** The computers at school are slow.

_____ **3.** Let's have Chinese food.

_____ **4.** The Chinese food at that restaurant is delicious.

_____ **5.** Robin eats the chocolate.

_____ **6.** The chocolate from Europe is very good.

_____ **7.** The apples in the bowl are old.

_____ **8.** Corey doesn't eat the apples.

_____ **9.** Teenagers love the music.

_____ **10.** I don't like the music he listens to in the car.

25 Practice

Complete the sentences with *the* or *X* (no article).

1. We need to buy ____________ tomatoes because ____________ tomatoes in the garden are still green.
2. Mick doesn't eat ____________ meat.
3. ____________ meat that they sell at that store isn't fresh.
4. ____________ money isn't very important to me.
5. He can barely live on ____________ money he makes.
6. I don't usually like ____________ carrots, but ____________ carrots in this salad are good.
7. Seung Wan dislikes ____________ cold weather. ____________ weather in his country is mild.
8. Mrs. Harris bought a bag of sugar this morning. She's using ____________ sugar in the bowl before she opens ____________ new bag.

9. Man Wen doesn't usually wear ____________ perfume, but ____________ perfume she's wearing tonight is very nice.

10. ____________ cars run on ____________ gasoline.

11. ____________ birds have ____________ feathers.

12. ____________ books in that shop are expensive.

13. I don't like ____________ homework, but ____________ homework we had last night was easy.

14. Jennifer loves shopping for ____________ clothes.

15. ____________ paper comes from ____________ trees.

16. Mr. Jacobs trimmed ____________ trees in his yard. They were too big.

26 Practice

Complete the sentences with your own ideas.

1. I *always listen to hip-hop* music. The music my parents listen to *is really old*.

2. I ________________ noise. The noise at my house ________________.

3. Traffic ________________. The traffic in my town ________________.

4. Animals ________________. The animals in the wildlife reserve ________________.

5. Friends ________________. The friends I have ________________.

6. Air pollution ________________. The air pollution in my country ________________.

7. Television shows ________________. The television shows I watch ________________.

8. Public transportation ________________. The public transportation in my town ________________.

SELF-TEST

A Choose the best answer, A, B, C, or D, to complete the sentence. Mark your answer by darkening the oval with the same letter.

1. The Herberts have three ________.

A. child
B. children
C. son
D. daughter

Ⓐ Ⓑ Ⓒ Ⓓ

2. Judith wants to go to the ________.

A. women's department
B. woman's department
C. womens' department
D. womans' department

Ⓐ Ⓑ Ⓒ Ⓓ

3. There isn't ________ money.

A. some
B. an
C. many
D. any

Ⓐ Ⓑ Ⓒ Ⓓ

4. She doesn't want ________ apple.

A. some
B. a
C. an
D. few

Ⓐ Ⓑ Ⓒ Ⓓ

5. I want a piece of ________.

A. milk
B. cake
C. toothpaste
D. soup

Ⓐ Ⓑ Ⓒ Ⓓ

6. It's dry and hot here. This place gets ________ rain.

A. little
B. a little
C. few
D. a few

Ⓐ Ⓑ Ⓒ Ⓓ

7. The doctors don't need ________ time.

A. a few
B. few
C. much
D. many

Ⓐ Ⓑ Ⓒ Ⓓ

8. Are you going to the store? I need a loaf of ________.

A. gasoline
B. bread
C. soap
D. toilet paper

Ⓐ Ⓑ Ⓒ Ⓓ

9. The ________ name is Dawn.

A. girls
B. girls'
C. girl
D. girl's

Ⓐ Ⓑ Ⓒ Ⓓ

10. Our assistant can go to the coffee shop. He has ________ time.

A. little
B. a little
C. few
D. a few

Ⓐ Ⓑ Ⓒ Ⓓ

B Find the underlined word or phrase, A, B, C, or D, that is incorrect. Mark your answer by darkening the oval with the same letter.

1. The couple (A) went to a lot of (B) partys (C) last year (D).

Ⓐ Ⓑ Ⓒ Ⓓ

2. I want to have (A) a little (B) fun (C), so I need a few (D) money.

Ⓐ Ⓑ Ⓒ Ⓓ

3. My sister's (A) names are (B) Amanda and Kelly. My brother's (C) name is (D) Nate.

Ⓐ Ⓑ Ⓒ Ⓓ

4. I'm making a few (A) progress (B). Now I understand most of (C) the homework (D).

Ⓐ Ⓑ Ⓒ Ⓓ

5. We've got a few (A) problems (B). We need to talk for a little (C) minutes (D).

Ⓐ Ⓑ Ⓒ Ⓓ

6. The men (A) needed some (B) information (C), and the counselor gave them an (D) advice.

Ⓐ Ⓑ Ⓒ Ⓓ

7. The volunteers bought (A) some (B) food (C), but they forgot the roll (D) of peanut butter.

Ⓐ Ⓑ Ⓒ Ⓓ

8. Charles's (A) opinion is like mine. That family needs a help (B) and some (C) happiness (D).

Ⓐ Ⓑ Ⓒ Ⓓ

9. My grandparents have a few (A) children (B) and grandchildren. They love babys (C) and young people (D).

Ⓐ Ⓑ Ⓒ Ⓓ

10. Clarissa doesn't usually (A) like the (B) mushrooms, but she liked the mushrooms (C) on the pizza (D) at lunch.

Ⓐ Ⓑ Ⓒ Ⓓ

UNIT 5 PRONOUNS

5a Subject and Object Pronouns

Student Book p. 102

1 Practice

Write *C* next to the sentence if the pronoun is correct. Write *I* if the pronoun is incorrect.

_____ **1.** She's going to tell they the secret.

_____ **2.** It's a secret.

_____ **3.** We know it.

_____ **4.** Her doesn't know it.

_____ **5.** Him is wearing new shoes.

_____ **6.** He gave us some directions.

_____ **7.** Them weren't clear.

_____ **8.** We got lost.

_____ **9.** It was difficult to find.

_____ **10.** I talked to he before we left.

_____ **11.** He told I the way.

2 Practice

Replace the underlined nouns with the subject and object pronouns.

1. Paul taught the students about the Gulf War.

   He taught them about it.

2. Luanne studied law before Luanne married Robert.

   ______________________________.

3. You and I are going to miss the bus.

   ______________________________.

4. Don saw you and me at the party.

   ______________________________.

5. Hannah drove Michael to the office.

   ______________________________.

6. The directions weren't clear to Laura and Rob.

   ______________________________.

3 Practice

Complete the sentences with subject or object pronouns.

A. Ted and Danielle wrote a report and ________(1) put ________(2) on the desk. I called ________(3) because I didn't find ________(4). Someone took ________(5). Ted and Danielle wrote the report again. ________(6) finished ________(7) at 4:00 and put ________(8) in a drawer. Then ________(9) locked ________(10).

B. Jeremy is going to a new school, but he doesn't know anyone yet. ________(1) decided to have a party, and yesterday ________(2) talked to some other students. Jeremy invited ________(3) to his apartment for the party. ________(4) came, and ________(5) had a good time.

C. Kate told the children a scary story, and now ________(1) are scared. ________(2) is really sorry she told ________(3) the story. ________(4) are afraid to go to bed, and ________(5) feels bad.

D. Mother to daughter:

Mother: Have you cleaned your room today?

Daughter: Yes, Mom. I cleaned ________(1) an hour ago.

Mother: What about the dishes?

Daughter: I put ________(2) away. Can I call Lydia now?

Mother: Not yet. ________(3)'re not finished. ________(4) need to make the bed. You can call ________(5) when ________(6)'re done.

5b Possessive Adjectives and Possessive Pronouns

Student Book p. 105

4 Practice

Rewrite the sentences using both forms of the possessive pronouns. In some cases, only one choice may be possible.

1. It's David's toy.

   It's his toy. It's his.

2. They're not Helen's cigarettes.

   ______________________________.

3. That's my and my wife's church.

   ______________________________.

4. It's not your turn! It's my turn.

   ______________________________.

5. That was my grandparents' business.

   ______________________________.

6. Mom: Whose dirty dishes are these?
   Son: They're not my dishes.

   ______________________________.

7. Your mom is a lot of fun.

   ______________________________.

8. He's not my and my husband's cat.

   ______________________________.

5 Practice

Read the article about the blues. Then write the underlined possessive pronouns as possessive adjectives and the possessive adjectives as possessive pronouns.

Many people believe that blues music has its roots in Africa. Slaves sang their songs (1) of loneliness, lost love, pain, and suffering and brought their musical heritage (2) to North America. Some people believe blues music is a combination of African melody and western tones.

The blues became popular to white audiences when white singers based their music (3) on the blues tradition. Elvis Presley sang "You Ain't Nothing But a Hound Dog," which Willie May "Big Mama" Thornton originally recorded in 1952. Her version (4) is a little bit different from Elvis's.

Some of the famous blues musicians from past and present are Muddy Waters, Bessie Smith, John Lee Hooker, Robert Johnson, to name only a few. Today, B.B. King is one of the most well-known blues guitarists to 20th century audiences. His guitar (5), Lucille, is almost as famous.

1. ____________________
2. ____________________
3. ____________________
4. ____________________
5. ____________________

5c Reflexive Pronouns

Student Book p. 107

6 Practice

Write *C* next to the sentence if the reflexive pronoun is correct. Write *I* if the reflexive pronoun is incorrect.

_____ **1.** He made it herself.

_____ **2.** We introduced ourselves.

_____ **3.** Jackie and John took care of it itself.

_____ **4.** I cut my hair by himself.

_____ **5.** You and Jean are going by yourselves.

_____ **6.** I just burned yourself on the pan.

_____ **7.** Rebecca didn't do her homework by herself.

_____ **8.** My friends and I enjoyed themselves.

_____ **9.** I taught myself how to sew.

_____ **10.** Michelle and Sarah are planning the conference themselves.

7 Practice

Complete the sentences with the correct reflexive pronoun.

1. Mother: What happened to the window?!

Son: I don't know.

Mother: Well, it didn't break _____________!

2. My daughter and son-in-law are building their own house and they're doing it _________________.

3. My best friend and I are planning to drive across the country by _________________ after we graduate.

4. Kurt: I'm hungry.

Melissa: There's some tuna salad in the refrigerator. Help _________________.

5. Marta and John: We're hungry.

   Todd: There's some pizza over there. Help ________________.

6. George taught ________________ how to play the guitar.

7. I'm doing this exercise by ________________.

8. They started their own business because they wanted to work for ________________.

9. Mother: Elizabeth! Dean! Stop fighting. If you don't behave ________________, we're not going to the park.

10. Leroy: Ouch!

    Shanya: What happened?

    Leroy: I hurt ________________.

11. Maria: What happened to Mr. Stevens?

    Sam: He cut ________________ while he was shaving.

12. Vicky: Why are you talking to ________________?

    Jim: I'm thinking out loud.

13. Giles: Who's that pretty girl over there?

    Charlie: That's my cousin, Susan. Go introduce ________________.

14. Douglas: Why are you walking so slowly?

    Joyce: I hurt ________________ while I was skiing.

15. Nick: Did Anna call the electrician yesterday?

    William: No, she fixed the problem ________________.

16. Thanks for dinner. We really enjoyed ________________.

17. Mandy: Wow, what's wrong with Ken? He looks terrible.

    Joe: I know. He isn't taking care of ________________.

18. I hate cleaning the kitchen. I want a house that will clean ________________.

19. Our cats clean ________________.

20. Jay: What happened to the radio? Why did it stop?

    Amber: I don't know. It turned ________________ off.

5d *Another, The Other, Other, Others,* and *The Others*

Student Book p. 110

8 Practice

Complete the sentences with *another* or *the other.*

1. Samantha: I need ________________ pencil.

   Bob: Here. I have two. I'll keep one, and you can have ________________.

2. Cesare: Would you like to dance?

   Betty: No, thanks. ________________ time.

3. There are only three songs before the club closes. I think I'm going to dance to two of them and sit down for ________________.

4. Renee: Would you like ________________ piece of cake?

   Mel: Sure. It's delicious.

5. There are two slices of cake left. I'm going to have one. Would you like ________________?

6. Ali has two sisters. One is in college and ________________ is in high school.

7. Hey. There were four bottles of water, and now there are only two. What happened to ________________ bottles?

8. Manicurist to customer:

   I finished with this hand. Please give me ________________.

9. Karen had an eye test. First the doctor looked at one eye, and then ________________.

10. Okay, here is the movie selection. There are three movies playing downtown. One is a scary movie, ________________ is a romantic comedy, and ________________ is a historical drama.

11. Kelly has two pairs of sunglasses, but one pair is broken, and she can't find ________________.

12. Our family grows apples. Here, please take one. Have ________________. We have a lot!

13. He took a step closer to me. Then, he took ________________, and ________________, and ________________ until I told him to stop.

9 Practice

Write *C* next to the sentence if *other, the other, others,* or *the others* is used correctly. Write *I* if *other, the other, others,* or *the others* is used incorrectly.

_____ **1.** I have some others ideas.

_____ **2.** The others students aren't finished.

_____ **3.** Other people are waiting to use the phone.

_____ **4.** I work well with others.

_____ **5.** I have a lot of friends. Some are men and the other are women.

10 Practice

Complete the sentences with *other, the other, others,* or *the others.*

1. Edward doesn't like college. Some classes are too easy, ____________ are too difficult.

2. The museum is showing three styles right now. One is impressionism, another is abstract realism, and a third is surrealism. I like impressionism, but ____________ don't interest me.

3. There are 13 students in my class. Seven of them are from Korea, four of them are from China, and ____________ are from Japan.

4. Some TV shows are good, and ____________ are not very funny.

5. My two favorite TV shows are on Sunday. One is on early, and ____________ is on late.

6. The art teacher liked some of the pieces, but he said ____________ pieces needed work.

11 Practice

Complete the sentences with *another, the other, others,* or *the others.*

A. One summer some friends of mine and I went on a backpacking trip. Two of us were women and ____________(1) were men. ____________(2) person wanted to come with us, but she couldn't. Three of us were from the United States, but ____________(3) woman was from England originally. We went hiking for a month in the mountains.

My mom told me that some of the neighbors were worried about us; that it was dangerous for 19-year-olds to go so far away alone, but ______________ (4) thought it was a great thing for us to do.

We had a wonderful time and we learned three important things. The first thing we learned was how to make group decisions. ______________ (5) thing we learned was how to be independent, and ______________ (6) thing we learned was that everything we needed we could carry on our backs.

B. One summer, my brother worked as a camp counselor in a summer camp. Some of the kids were from small towns, and ______________ (1) were from the city. He had five boys in his cabin. One of them was a troublemaker, but ______________ (2) were very sweet.

The camp was on a lake, and my brother was a lifeguard. There were two of them. ______________ (3) lifeguard, John, was lazy. One time, John didn't see that one of the boys was in trouble, and my brother jumped in the water to save him. ______________ (4) time, John didn't come to work all day, so my brother had to watch all the boys while they were swimming.

5e *One* and *Ones*

Student Book p. 113

12 Practice

Complete the sentences with *one* or *ones*.

A. Anya: Which section are you in?

Terry: The last ______________ (1), with Dr. Hardey.

Anya: Did you buy your books?

Terry: I bought the ______________ (2) on the list.

B. Steven: What do you think of the candy?

Malcom: The black ______________ (1) are good, but I don't like the red ______________ (2).

C. Leslie: Which cars did you like?

Claudia: I liked the small, fast ______________.
(1)

Leslie: Which color car did you choose?

Claudia: I picked the dark green ______________.
(2)

Leslie: How about the stereo?

Claudia: I ordered the best ______________.
(3)

Leslie: Have you got the insurance?

Claudia: Not yet, but I'm thinking about the two basic ______________.
(4)

13 Practice

Complete the sentences with *one, ones, some, it,* or *them*.

1. I need a cup of coffee. Would you like ____________, too?
2. Mike: Those pants are dirty.

   Patrick: I don't have any other ____________.
3. Jessica: Let's go shopping for new pants.

   Ellen: Good idea. I need ____________.
4. Those grapes look good. Let's get ____________.
5. Paul: Have you got a computer for school? You'll need ____________.

   Theresa: Yes, I have. I'm taking ____________ with me tomorrow.
6. Paula: Which flowers do you like?

   Jeannie: I like the white ____________.
7. Kirk: Here are your groceries.

   Vivian: Put ____________ on the counter.
8. Rachel: I left my purse at the bank.

   Frank: Are you going to go get ____________?
9. Are those mints? May I have ____________?
10. I can't find my pen. Where is ____________?
11. Katerina painted a few new paintings this year. I really like the ____________ she just finished last week.

12. Gene: Here's your mail.

Mei: Thanks. Could you put ____________ on the table?

13. Sara: Did you look at apartments last weekend?

Henri: Yes, the last ____________ we looked at was okay.

14. Jody likes the new car, but I like the old ____________ better.

5f Indefinite Pronouns

Student Book p. 113

14 Practice

Write *C* next to the sentence if the indefinite pronoun is correct. Write *I* if the indefinite pronoun is incorrect.

_____ 1. He doesn't like anybody.

_____ 2. There isn't nothing in the refrigerator.

_____ 3. Everyone's coming tomorrow.

_____ 4. Anyone is at the door.

_____ 5. The children don't have anything to do.

_____ 6. Nobody called while we were out.

_____ 7. Yvonne isn't going nowhere.

_____ 8. I called but someone didn't answer.

15 Practice

Underline the correct indefinite pronouns in parentheses.

1. Police officer 1: What happened here?

Police officer 2: I don't know. There were a lot of people here, but (no one / anyone) saw anything.

Police officer 1: Who did you question?

Police officer 2: I've asked (everyone / anyone) here.

2. Ngan: I don't remember where I parked my car. I can't find it, and I've looked (somewhere / everywhere).

   Seung: Okay, let's ask (anyone / someone) to help us.

3. Teacher: Why aren't you working?

   Student: I don't have (nothing / anything) to do.

4. Max: What's wrong?

   Dana: (Something / Everything). I hate my job, my car doesn't work, and I never get to see my friends.

5. Hello? Is (anybody / nobody) home?

6. Carl: Are you okay?

   Michael: No, I can't feel (something / anything) in my hand.

7. Doctor: How did you hurt yourself?

   Bill: I'm not sure. I was working out, but I didn't do (everything / anything) differently. (Something / Everything) is wrong, though. It hurts to walk.

8. Roommate 1: I'm leaving. (Something / Nothing) you say will make me stay.

   Roommate 2: Why? I didn't do (anything / nothing) wrong!

9. Roommate 1: I'm going to the store. Do you need (everything / anything)?

   Roommate 2: Nope. I have (everything / anything) I need.

10. Mom: You're late for school. (Everyone / Someone) is already on the bus.

    Jennifer: I can't find my backpack (anywhere / nowhere).

SELF-TEST

A Choose the best answer, A, B, C, or D, to complete the sentence. Mark your answer by darkening the oval with the same letter.

1. These are _______.

   A. our
   B. ours
   C. your
   D. their

   Ⓐ Ⓑ Ⓒ Ⓓ

2. Adrienne cut _______ on the knife.

   A. herself
   B. ourselves
   C. themselves
   D. myself

   Ⓐ Ⓑ Ⓒ Ⓓ

3. _______ is wearing silver earrings.

   A. Hers
   B. Her
   C. Anyone
   D. Everyone

   Ⓐ Ⓑ Ⓒ Ⓓ

4. Digital cameras are good, but old film _______ are better.

   A. one
   B. the one
   C. ones
   D. another

   Ⓐ Ⓑ Ⓒ Ⓓ

5. Yum. This ice cream is good. Would you like _______ bowl?

   A. another
   B. some
   C. it
   D. the other

   Ⓐ Ⓑ Ⓒ Ⓓ

6. The tea is in the kitchen. Please help _______.

   A. mine
   B. theirs
   C. myself
   D. yourselves

   Ⓐ Ⓑ Ⓒ Ⓓ

7. My two sisters are older. One lives in Seattle, and _______ is in New York.

   A. another
   B. some
   C. it
   D. the other

   Ⓐ Ⓑ Ⓒ Ⓓ

8. There were ten complaints. Four were about our sales people, three were about our prices, and _______ were about the product.

   A. another
   B. some
   C. the others
   D. the other

   Ⓐ Ⓑ Ⓒ Ⓓ

9. Tara didn't see _______.

   A. someone
   B. nobody
   C. nothing
   D. anyone

   Ⓐ Ⓑ Ⓒ Ⓓ

10. Whose watches are these? _______.

    A. Mine
    B. My
    C. Hers watches
    D. Her

    Ⓐ Ⓑ Ⓒ Ⓓ

B **Find the underlined word or phrase, A, B, C, or D, that is incorrect. Mark your answer by darkening the oval with the same letter.**

1. I'm (A) not sure if he (B) is going to come, but she (C) sister is going to come (D).

(A) (B) (C) (D)

2. Javier and Kimberley (A) have (B) a car. The blue one (C) is their (D).

(A) (B) (C) (D)

3. Jack built his (A) company by yourself (B). Nobody (C) helped him (D).

(A) (B) (C) (D)

4. Anyone (A) took the bananas. I (B) only ate one (C) and the others (D) were on the counter.

(A) (B) (C) (D)

5. I looked anywhere (A). Someone (B) took my keys (C). They (D) were on the dining room table.

(A) (B) (C) (D)

6. Let's (A) get some tomatoes (B). Ones (C) over there look good (D).

(A) (B) (C) (D)

7. It's (A) not your (B) bag, it's my (C). Yours (D) is on the floor.

(A) (B) (C) (D)

8. Which (A) lotion do you like (B)? This one (C) or that ones (D)?

(A) (B) (C) (D)

9. Terrel made it (A) by himself (B). Anyone (C) helped him (D).

(A) (B) (C) (D)

10. The glasses (A) are theirs (B), but the dishes (C) are our (D).

(A) (B) (C) (D)

UNIT 6 THE PRESENT AND PAST PERPECT

6a The Present Perfect

Student Book p. 122

1 Practice

Complete the following chart. Use the simple present tense, the simple past tense, and the past participle of the verbs.

Verb	Simple Present Tense	Simple Past Tense	Past Participle
1. *be*	*is, am, are*		
2.		*ate*	
3.			*given*
4. *drink*			
5.			*gotten*
6.		*had*	
7.		*knew*	
8. *put*			
9.		*read*	
10.			*seen*
11.		*took*	
12. *write*			

2 Practice

Complete the sentences with the present perfect tense of the verbs in parentheses. Then complete the questions and write answers.

A. Tom: I am so lazy today. I have so much to do, and I (not, do) ________ (1) much. I (not, make) ________ (2) the bed, and I (not, take) ________ (3) out the garbage. I (not, call) ________ (4) my professor or (finish) ________ (5) my paper yet, and it's already 3:00 P.M.!

a. (call) ______________ Tom ______________ his professor yet?

b. ____.

c. (get) ______________ Tom ______________ dressed yet?

d. ____.

e. What (do) ______________ Tom ______________ today?

f. ____.

B. Interviewer: Tell me about your work experience. What (do) ______________ (1) you ______________ (1)?

Lewis: Well, I (study) ______________ (2) three languages and (travel) ______________ (3) around the world. I (be) ______________ (4) to Moscow twice. I (work) ______________ (5) on many sales teams, and I (have) ______________ (6) a lot of experience working with people.

a. (be) ______________ he ______________ a waiter?

b. ____.

c. (travel) ______________ he ______________ a lot?

d. ____.

e. What other experience (have) ______________ he ______________?

f. ____.

C. Monique: (finish) ______________ (1) you ______________ (1) the assignment?

Scott: Yes, I (have) ______________ (2). I (not, sleep) ______________ (3) for two nights, but it's finally done! What about you? (finish) ______________ (4) you ______________ (4) it?

Monique: No, I (not, have) ______________ (5).

a. (finish) ______________ Scott ______________ the assignment?

b. ____.

c. (finish) ______________ Monique ______________ the assignment?

d. ____.

D. Terry had a very different life 10 years ago. He ate too much, was single, watched a lot of TV, and didn't have any friends. He was very unhappy. He quit overeating 10 years ago, and he (not, watch) ______________ (1) too much TV in 10 years. He (start) ______________ (2) exercising, and he (make) ______________ (3) new friends. He (be) ______________ (4) married to his second wife for seven years. His children (become) ______________ (5) closer to him. He (change) ______________ (6) his life dramatically, and today, Terry is a very happy man.

a. (stop) ______________ Terry ______________ overeating?

b. ____.

c. (be) ______________ he ______________ single for seven years?

d. ____.

e. What (happen) ______________ to Terry and his children?

f. ____.

g. (change) ______________ he ______________ his life?

h. ____.

6b *For* and *Since*

Student Book p. 127

3 Practice

Write *for* or *since* for the following phrases.

_____ **a.** my last vacation

_____ **b.** three months

_____ **c.** 50 years

_____ **d.** last week

_____ **e.** ten minutes

_____ **f.** 10:00 A.M.

_____ **g.** I graduated from college

_____ **h.** Saturday night

_____ **i.** this morning

_____ **j.** a few days

_____ **k.** half a day

_____ **l.** 2000

_____ **m.** a long time

_____ **n.** last night

_____ **o.** Tuesday

_____ **p.** we started this exercise

_____ **q.** a year

_____ **r.** seven days

_____ **s.** breakfast

4 Practice

Write *C* next to the sentence if *for* or *since* is used correctly. Write *I* if *for* or *since* is used incorrectly.

_____ **1.** Kathy's worked in the hotel since 1998.

_____ **2.** Todd's had a headache for 1:00.

_____ **3.** Jeannie's been a teacher for eight years.

_____ **4.** Karl hasn't smoked since a year.

_____ **5.** Brian's had long hair for nine years.

_____ **6.** They've lived in Singapore since 2001.

_____ **7.** I haven't seen you since my last birthday!

_____ **8.** Laurel hasn't seen her cousins for last year.

_____ **9.** Choi hasn't been to Korea since he was 20 years old.

_____ **10.** Donna and her parents haven't seen each other for Tuesday.

5 Practice

Complete the sentences about you, your parents, and your friends.

1. I ______________________________ since this morning.
2. I ______________________________ for 24 hours.
3. I ____________________ since ____________________.
4. I (not) ____________________ for ____________________.
5. My parents ____________________ since ____________________.
6. My friend(s) ____________________ for ____________________.
7. My English class ____________________ since ____________________.

6c *Ever* and *Never*

Student Book p. 128

6 Practice

Write *C* next to the sentence if *ever* or *never* is used correctly. Write *I* if *ever* or *never* is used incorrectly.

_____ 1. We've ever seen that movie.

_____ 2. Jana's never been married.

_____ 3. Have the Washingtons ever been to Toronto?

_____ 4. No, they never have.

_____ 5. Elaine's ever met the neighbors.

7 Practice

Write questions and answers using the prompts.

1. ever/be in a car accident

   Have you ever been in a car accident?

   Yes, I have, but I was okay.

2. ever/do military service

   ______________________________?

   No, ____________________, but I will next year.

3. ever/break a leg

____?

No, ____________________, but I've broken my arm.

4. ever/live in a dormitory

____?

Yes, ____________________. I lived in one my first year at college.

5. ever/play basketball

____?

Yes, ____________________. I just played yesterday!

6. ever/grow a beard

____?

No, ____________________. I'm a woman!

7. ever/study calculus

____?

No, ____________________. I wasn't very good at math in school.

8. ever/swim in the ocean

____?

No, ____________________. I don't know how to swim.

9. ever/break a mirror

____?

Yes, ____________________. I dropped it while I was moving.

10. ever/use a typewriter

____________________________?

No, ____________________. What's a typewriter?

8 Practice

Write questions and answers about yourself with *have you ever* and the prompts.

1. get a driver's license

   Have you ever gotten a driver's license?

   No, I haven't.

2. bake a cake

   ______________________________?

   ______________________________.

3. go to another country

   ______________________________?

   ______________________________.

4. speak English in the United States

   ______________________________?

   ______________________________.

5. study the present perfect before

   ______________________________?

   ______________________________.

6. have a pet

   ______________________________?

   ______________________________.

7. order a pizza

   ______________________________?

   ______________________________.

8. buy a house

   ______________________________?

   ______________________________.

9. go surfing

   ______________________________?

   ______________________________.

10. wear makeup

____?

____.

11. pierce your nose or eyebrow

____?

____.

12. do magic tricks

____?

____.

6d *Already, Yet,* and *Just*

Student Book p. 131

9 Practice

Underline the correct words in parentheses.

1. Has she arrived (just / yet)?
2. Yes, she's (just / yet) gotten here.
3. We've (already / yet) eaten. Are you hungry?
4. Yes, I am. I haven't eaten (already / yet).
5. Steve hasn't called you (just / yet)?
6. He's (just / yet) sent you email.
7. The children haven't seen the pirate movie (just / yet).
8. My kids have (already / yet) seen it.
9. Have you gone to the dentist (yet / just)?
10. No, not (just / yet).

10 Practice

Write sentences using the present perfect with *already* or *yet* and the prompts.

1. invent flying cars

   People haven't invented flying cars yet.

2. discover radio waves

   ______________________________.

3. find cure for colds

   ______________________________.

4. build cities on the moon

   ______________________________.

5. discover electricity

   ______________________________.

6. make robots

   ______________________________.

7. find answer to world hunger

   ______________________________.

8. make airplanes

   ______________________________.

9. (your choice)

   ______________________________.

10. (your choice)

   ______________________________.

11 Practice

When Belinda was 10 years old, she made a list of things she wanted to do in her life. She's already done some of them, but she hasn't done others yet. Read the list and write sentences using the present perfect and *already* or *yet*.

Things I want to do
1. finish college ✔
2. find a good job
3. see the pyramids in Egypt
4. see the Great Wall of China ✔
5. parachute out of an airplane ✔
6. climb Mt. Everest
7. move to California ✔
8. become a famous singer

1. *She has already finished college*.
2. ______.
3. ______.
4. ______.
5. ______.
6. ______.
7. ______.
8. ______.

12 Practice

Write five goals you had for your life when you were 10 years old.

Example: *When I was 10, I wanted to study ballet.*

1. ______.
2. ______.
3. ______.
4. ______.
5. ______.

Read your list and write sentences using the present perfect and *already* or *yet*.

Example: I haven't studied ballet yet.

1. ______________________________.
2. ______________________________.
3. ______________________________.
4. ______________________________.
5. ______________________________.

6e The Simple Past OR the Present Perfect

Student Book p. 133

13 Practice

Read the sentences. Write *P* next to the sentence if the action is in the past or is finished. Write *N* (for *now*) if the action is still true in the present.

_____ 1. They got married two weeks ago.

_____ 2. I didn't go to the wedding.

_____ 3. Have they come back from their honeymoon?

_____ 4. No, they've been in Fiji for two weeks.

_____ 5. I've already gotten a postcard from them.

_____ 6. I got it two days ago.

_____ 7. Her parents haven't heard from them yet.

_____ 8. They've known each other since they were in high school.

_____ 9. The wedding was beautiful.

_____ 10. I haven't bought them a present yet.

14 Practice

Read the sentences. Then write a sentence using the present perfect tense.

1. Three years ago, Cindy bought a new truck. She still has her truck today.

   She's had her truck for three years.

2. Serena and Jacob arrived in Canada in 1998. They're still there.

   ______________________________.

3. Jim got his dog in February. He still has him.

____.

4. Jan stopped smoking six years ago. She still doesn't smoke.

____.

5. My country became independent in 1978. It's still independent.

____.

6. The movie started at 7:00. We're still in the theater.

____.

7. Kevin's best friend and Kevin had an argument three months ago. They still don't talk to each other.

____.

8. Mona dyed her hair for the first time a few years ago. She still dyes her hair.

____.

9. Matthew got depressed after his mother died. He's still depressed today.

____.

10. Jocelyn started piano lessons when she was 10 years old. She still plays piano today.

____.

15 Practice

Complete the sentences with the simple past or present perfect of the verbs in parentheses.

A. Alan: (buy) ______(1)______ you ______(1)______ tickets yet?

P.J.: Yes, I ______(2)______. I (get) ______(3)______ them last night. I (be) ______(4)______ lucky. I (get) ______(5)______ the last two tickets.

Alan: (pay) ______(6)______ I ______(6)______ you yet?

P.J.: No, you ______(7)______.

B. Vicky: (see) ______(1)______ you ______(1)______ the office?

Shelly: No, I ______(2)______. Why?

Vicky: Someone (paint) ______(3)______ it bright yellow over the weekend!

Shelly: Oh, no!

C. Teacher: Please hand in your assignment.

Student: I (not, finish) ________ (1) yet.

Teacher: Why not?

Student: My computer (crash) ________ (2) last night.

D. Judy: (stop) ________ (1) it ________ (1) raining?

Peter: Yes, it ________ (2). It (stop) ________ (3) about an hour ago.

E. Antonio: Are you hungry? (eat) ________ (1) you ________ (1)?

Serena: Yes, I ________ (2). Thanks anyway.

F. Jae: This looks like a nice restaurant.

Isabella: It is. I (eat) ________ (1) here before.

Jae: Oh, when?

Isabella: I (be) ________ (2) here about a year ago.

Jae: (be) ________ (3) the food good?

Isabella: Yes, it ________ (4).

G. Jon: Ouch, my tooth really hurts!

Celine: (call) ________ (1) you ________ (1) the dentist yet?

Jon: Yes, I (call) ________ (2) a little while ago, and I (make) ________ (3) an appointment.

H. Sean: How long (work) ________ (1) he ________ (1) here?

Keenan: I think he (be) ________ (2) here for a long time.

Sean: When (start) ________ (3) he ________ (3)?

Keenan: I think he (come) ________ (4) here about 12 years ago.

16 Practice

Read the following questions about your country and/or city. Answer them using the present perfect and *for, since, never,* or *always*.

1. Is your country independent?

Yes, my country has been independent since 1965. (OR)

My country has always been independent. (OR)

My country has never had independence.

2. Does your country compete in the World Cup?

____.

3. Does your country use nuclear power?

____.

4. Do women make as much money as men in your country?

____.

5. Are there no-smoking sections in restaurants in your city?

____.

6. Do men do military service in your country?

____.

6f The Present Perfect Progressive

Student Book p. 135

17 Practice

Complete the sentences with the present perfect progressive of the verbs in parentheses.

1. Jessica: What (do) ______________ you ______________?

   Your teeth are blue!

   Michael: I (chew) ______________ some bubble gum.

2. Receptionist: Oh, I didn't see you! How long (sit) ______________ you ______________ there?

   Kate: I (wait) ______________ for 90 minutes.

3. This is Janice's favorite painting. She (work) ______________ on it for eight months.

4. My friend's mom (make) ______________ jam for over 30 years.

5. Carole: What are you thinking about?

   Tom: Lunch.

   Carole: How long (think) ______________ you ______________ about lunch?

   Tom: All morning. My stomach (growl) ______________ since 10:00!

6. She (cry) ______________ since she heard the bad news.

7. Terry: Hi, how are you? What (do) ________________ you ________________?

   Cindy: I (work) ________________ a lot, and I (teach) ________________ a night class. I (also, go) ________________ to a yoga class.

8. Traffic is really bad. We (sit) ________________ here for 20 minutes. Maureen (get) ________________ worried she's going to be late for work.

9. Linda: Wow, it's quiet.

   Craig: Yes, the kids (sleep) ________________ for almost two hours.

10. Nicole and Doug (attend) ________________ college since they finished high school.

11. So many things (happen) ________________ since we last saw you! Max (learn) ________________ how to snowboard. The baby (walk) ________________ a lot. Larry (make) ________________ more money, and I (lose) ________________ weight.

12. My wife and I (think) ________________ about moving. We (have) ________________ trouble with our neighbors, so we (think) ________________ about buying a new house.

18 Practice

Read the following information. Write a sentence using the present perfect progressive tense.

1. Greg started watching TV three hours ago. He's still watching TV now.

   *Greg's been watching TV for three hours*________________.

2. Chandra started smoking when she was 17 years old. She still smokes now.

   ________________________________.

3. Jill got on the phone after she came home. She's still talking on the phone now.

   ________________________________.

4. Shawna started taking vitamins a year ago. She still takes them now.

   ________________________________.

5. Bob got a job delivering pizzas nine months ago. He still delivers them now.

   ________________________________.

6. Carlos started shopping at 9:00 this morning, and he's still shopping now.

____.

7. The boys started playing video games when they got home from school. They're still playing games now.

____.

8. Gus started yawning about 20 minutes ago. He's yawning right now.

____.

6g The Present Perfect OR the Present Perfect Progressive

Student Book p. 137

19 Practice

Read the sentences. Write *P* next to the sentence if the action is in the past or is finished. Write *N* (for *now*) if the action is still happening in the present.

_____ 1. The class has finished the assignment.

_____ 2. My friends' class has been working on it for 30 minutes.

_____ 3. Kenji's gone home.

_____ 4. Mary and Susan have been traveling for 10 days.

_____ 5. Reuben's eaten dinner.

_____ 6. The children have been eating dinner for half an hour.

_____ 7. Elisa's been working since she was 14 years old.

_____ 8. Susan's worked in construction.

_____ 9. My daughter's gone to sleep.

_____ 10. My dad's been wearing the same coat for 15 years!

20 Practice

Complete the sentences with the present perfect or the present perfect progressive of the verbs in parentheses. More than one answer may be possible.

A. Arnold: They (build) ____________ (1) that apartment complex for 18 months. Why (take) ____________ (2) it ____________ (2) so long?

Maria: They (have) ____________ (3) a few problems. The city (not, give) ____________ (4) the owners permission to put in a pool, and they (change) ______________ (5) architects twice. The builders also (not, receive) ______________ (6) all the materials they need.

B. Martha: What's the matter?

Joe: I (sit) ______________ (1) at my computer all day, and I (not, finish) ______________ (2) my project yet.

Martha: Why?

Joe: Well, it (crash) ______________ (3) a couple times, and the printer (not, work) ______________ (4) since I installed it.

C. Boss: What (do) ______________ (1) you ______________ (1)? I (wait) ______________ (2) for your report for an hour.

Employee: I (talk) ______________ (3) with the team, and we (make) ______________ (4) notes.

D. Sylvia: How long (work) ______________ (1) you ______________ (1) here?

Lauren: I (work) ______________ (2) here for about six months, but I (cut) ______________ (3) hair for 13 years. I really like this salon. I (learn) ______________ (4) some new techniques from my coworkers.

E. Anya (start) ______________ (1) working out, and she feels great. She (stop) ______________ (2) going to the aerobics class, but she (do) ______________ (3) yoga for a long time. She (try) ______________ (4) a few other classes, but she likes yoga the best. She (practice) ______________ (5) yoga for three years.

F. Daphne is an English teacher. Since September, Daphne (work) ______(1)______ with young adults, and she (teach) ______(2)______ other young teachers how to teach. She (have) ______(3)______ a lot of experience in her field. She (learn) ______(4)______ a lot from her students, and she (visit) ______(5)______ many places around the world. She (study) ______(6)______ Japanese and Spanish.

G. The city government (try) ______(1)______ to change some social problems. They (already, provide) ______(2)______ 600 new jobs and (give) ______(3)______ money to educational programs. They (work) ______(4)______ on a theater program for teenagers from low-income homes for a couple weeks.

21 Practice

Read the following information. Write a sentence using the present perfect progressive or present perfect tense. More than one answer may be possible.

1. Adam saw that movie two weeks ago, last week, and again last night.

   He's seen that movie three times.

2. Andy took off his glasses last night. He's not wearing them now.

   He hasn't been wearing his glasses since last night.

3. The LeGrands moved here in 1990. They still live here now.

   ______________________________.

4. Chris lay down in bed at 2:00. He's still lying there now.

   ______________________________.

5. Dori and Roberto got married in 2002. They're still married now.

   ______________________________.

6. Donny went to Italy in 1999. He went again in 2003.

   ______________________________.

7. We sent him email at 8:30 and again at midnight.

   ______________________________.

6h The Past Perfect

Student Book p. 140

22 Practice

Complete the sentences using the past perfect or the simple past tense.

1. She (already, close) ______________________ the car door when she (see) ______________ that she (leave) ______________ her keys inside.
2. When the baby (start) ______________ to cry, Eileen and Mike (just, fall) ______________________ asleep.
3. Rachel (be) ___________ absent a week before she (tell) ___________ her teachers.
4. Ing Chul (already, leave) ______________________ when Javier (come) ________ looking for her.
5. When the police (arrive) ______________, the thieves (leave) ______________.
6. The politician (be) ______________ an actor before he (become) ___________ involved in politics.
7. When their daughter (decide) ______________ to take music lessons, her parents (already, sell) ______________________ their piano.
8. My wife and I (not, finish) ______________________ watching the movie when someone in front of us (shout) ___________ out the ending.
9. Luckily, Miriam and Janet (get) ______________ to the dock before the ship (leave) ___________.
10. The frantic mother (already, call) ___________________ 911 when her son (walk) ______________ in the door.

23 Practice

Read each pair of sentences. Decide which action happened first and which happened second. Combine them into sentences using the past perfect or the simple past tense.

1. The car broke down. It started to rain.

   It had started to rain when the car broke down.

2. We left. He called.

   ____.

3. We didn't go very far. The car broke down.

____.

4. We realized we left the cell phone in the trunk. We looked for the cell phone.

____.

5. We were in the car for two hours. The tow truck arrived.

____.

6. We got home. We realized we had lost the keys, so we slept in the car.

____.

24 Practice

Answer the questions using the past perfect tense.

1. Why did the company go out of business?

   One of the managers had stolen a lot of money.

2. Why didn't she eat lunch?

   ____.

3. Why didn't you answer the phone last night?

   ____.

4. Why was your roommate angry when you brought home a pizza last night?

   ____.

5. Why did Mr. McClean get the job in Australia?

   ____.

6. Why did the sales team have to redo their project?

   ____.

7. Why did Kelly get that reward?

   ____.

8. Why did the Browns adopt the two children?

   ____.

25 Practice

Complete the sentences with your own ideas. Use the present progressive or the simple past tense.

1. ______________________________ when the phone rang.
2. They'd already put out the fire when ______________________________.
3. Vince and Cheryl ______________________ when we visited them in France.
4. I hadn't seen Luanne in a long time before ______________________.
5. When we got married, ______________________________.

6i The Past Perfect Progressive

Student Book p. 142

26 Practice

Read the sentences. Write *P* next to the sentence if the action is in the past or is finished. Write *N* (for *now*) if the action is still in progress in the present.

_____ **1.** Our neighbors have been traveling for two weeks now.

_____ **2.** They'd been working very hard.

_____ **3.** The software company has been growing quickly.

_____ **4.** It had been producing 1,000 units a day.

_____ **5.** My grandparents have already eaten.

_____ **6.** They ate at 7:00 this morning.

_____ **7.** Mr. Leier has been teaching art history for a long time.

_____ **8.** The Lees have been married for 30 years.

_____ **9.** Michelle hadn't been working for her family's business for very long.

_____ **10.** She'd found another job.

27 Practice

Complete the sentences using the past perfect progressive or the simple past of the verbs in parentheses.

1. They (work) ____________________ for five days before they (hear) ______________ that the project (cancel) ______________.
2. Before she finally (leave) ______________, she (wait) ____________________ for 45 minutes for him to arrive.

3. Wayne (wear) ______________________ the same boots for 15 years before his son (throw) _______________ them away.
4. When it (start) _______________ to rain, Min (wash) ______________________ his car for 45 minutes.
5. The two sides (fight) ______________________ for a while before they (learn) _______________ the war (be) _______________ over.
6. My aunt (live) ______________________ in Australia for 10 years before she (see) _______________ a koala bear.
7. Before the owner finally (turn) _______________ it off, the car alarm (go) ______________________ off for 30 minutes.
8. When the earthquake (hit) _______________, we (not, sit) ______________________ in the restaurant very long.
9. When you (call) _______________ me, I (just, think) ______________________ about you!
10. The team (have) ______________________ a good time when the accident (happen) _______________.

28 Practice

Complete the sentences with the simple past or the past perfect progressive.

1. I'd been doing this exercise for ______________________ when ______________________.
2. Last night I'd been sleeping for ______________________ when ______________________.
3. My parents ______________________ before I left for school yesterday.
4. When ______________________, my best friend ______________________.
5. Before ______________________, my grandmother ______________________.

SELF-TEST

A Choose the best answer, A, B, C, or D, to complete the sentence. Mark your answer by darkening the oval with the same letter.

1. Fran and Charles _______ each other in four years.

A. didn't see Ⓐ Ⓑ Ⓒ Ⓓ
B. haven't seen
C. haven't been seeing
D. seen

2. We've been here _______ an hour.

A. since Ⓐ Ⓑ Ⓒ Ⓓ
B. already
C. yet
D. for

3. Hetty's _______ taken the photographs.

A. since Ⓐ Ⓑ Ⓒ Ⓓ
B. already
C. yet
D. for

4. My grandfather hasn't made dinner _______.

A. since Ⓐ Ⓑ Ⓒ Ⓓ
B. already
C. yet
D. for

5. They _______ many problems with the new telephone system.

A. 've had Ⓐ Ⓑ Ⓒ Ⓓ
B. had been
C. has had
D. has been having

6. Her hands were sore because she _______ for four hours.

A. has been typing Ⓐ Ⓑ Ⓒ Ⓓ
B. has typed
C. had been typing
D. have been typing

7. Before the bus arrived, Brian and Kumiko _______ talking.

A. has finished Ⓐ Ⓑ Ⓒ Ⓓ
B. have finished
C. hasn't finished
D. had finished

8. He _______ divorced before he met his second wife.

A. has been Ⓐ Ⓑ Ⓒ Ⓓ
B. had been
C. has been divorcing
D. have been

9. Hiroyuki and Thomas _______ since last night. They are almost finished.

A. have Ⓐ Ⓑ Ⓒ Ⓓ
B. have worked
C. worked
D. have been working

10. Ray's _______ done the washing.

A. since Ⓐ Ⓑ Ⓒ Ⓓ
B. already
C. yet
D. for

B Find the underlined word or phrase, A, B, C, or D, that is incorrect. Mark your answer by darkening the oval with the same letter.

1. Dr. Randy <u>has</u> (A) <u>been</u> (B) a dentist <u>since</u> (C) 12 years. He<u>'s been working</u> (D) in San Francisco for a long time.

   Ⓐ Ⓑ Ⓒ Ⓓ

2. His son had <u>already</u> (A) <u>brush</u> (B) his teeth <u>when</u> (C) I <u>made</u> (D) some hot chocolate.

   Ⓐ Ⓑ Ⓒ Ⓓ

3. The owners <u>have</u> (A) <u>knew</u> (B) about the problem with the roof <u>since</u> (C) <u>the winter</u> (D).

   Ⓐ Ⓑ Ⓒ Ⓓ

4. Ed has <u>yet</u> (A) <u>gone</u> (B) to bed. He's been <u>sleeping</u> (C) <u>for</u> (D) a couple hours.

   Ⓐ Ⓑ Ⓒ Ⓓ

5. Some of the students <u>didn't</u> (A) <u>felt</u> (B) well <u>since</u> (C) they <u>ate</u> (D) breakfast.

   Ⓐ Ⓑ Ⓒ Ⓓ

6. The author <u>has</u> (A) <u>already</u> (B) finished college <u>before</u> (C) he <u>wrote</u> (D) his first book.

   Ⓐ Ⓑ Ⓒ Ⓓ

7. He<u>'s come</u> (A) home <u>yet</u> (B). He<u>'d called</u> (C) before he <u>left</u> (D) the office.

   Ⓐ Ⓑ Ⓒ Ⓓ

8. The company <u>had</u> (A) <u>decide</u> (B) to give Monique a better position when <u>she</u> (C) <u>found</u> (D) a new job.

   Ⓐ Ⓑ Ⓒ Ⓓ

9. It's <u>been</u> (A) <u>snowing</u> (B) <u>for</u> (C) the morning. I've <u>gone</u> (D) outside three times.

   Ⓐ Ⓑ Ⓒ Ⓓ

10. The team has <u>been winning</u> (A) the championship <u>three times</u> (B). They <u>hadn't won</u> (C) a game <u>before</u> (D) 1999.

   Ⓐ Ⓑ Ⓒ Ⓓ

UNIT 7 QUESTIONS AND PHRASAL VERBS

7a Yes/No Questions and Short Answers

Student Book p. 150

1 Practice

Following is an interview with a retired international sales manager. Answer the questions.

1. Do you have a few minutes to talk?

   Yes, ___I do___.

2. Are you still an international sales manager?

   No, ________________.

3. Were you a marketing manager for your company?

   No, ________________. I was always in sales.

4. Did you travel a lot?

   Yes, ________________.

5. Did you work only in Europe?

   No, ________________.

6. Have you been to Korea?

   Yes, ________________. I've been there many times. I met my husband there.

7. Is your husband Korean?

   Yes, ________________.

8. Does he work?

   Yes, ________________. He's a stockbroker.

9. Can you speak Korean now?

   Yes, ________________.

10. Are you thinking of returning to sales?

    No, ________________.

11. Should we take a break now?

    Yes, ________________.

2 Practice

Read the questions and write answers to them.

1. Are there five colors in a rainbow?

   ______________________________.

2. Can giraffes fly?

   ______________________________.

3. Had people used phones before they used email?

   ______________________________.

4. Have doctors discovered a cure for AIDS?

   ______________________________.

5. Was Lady Diana Spencer from Germany?

   ______________________________.

6. Could women vote 20 years ago in the United States?

   ______________________________.

7. Was Beethoven from El Salvador?

   ______________________________.

8. Should people speed up at red lights?

   ______________________________.

9. Does popcorn grow on trees?

   ______________________________.

10. It is usually warm in Florida?

    ______________________________.

11. Do we use keys in locks?

    ______________________________.

12. Will people live on other planets in the future?

    ______________________________.

3 Practice

Answer the questions about yourself.

1. Do you like English? ______________________.
2. Can you play the guitar? ______________________.
3. Must we help other people? ______________________.
4. Should we study other cultures? ______________________.
5. Must all students attend college? ______________________.
6. Would you like some tea now? ______________________.
7. Are you a happy person? ______________________.
8. Do you smoke? ______________________.
9. Could you do cartwheels when you were younger? ______________________.
10. Can you do cartwheels now? ______________________.
11. Is your mom a good cook? ______________________.
12. Is your dad a good cook? ______________________.
13. Have you ever been in a car accident? ______________________.

4 Practice

Write questions about yourself based on the answers.

1. *Will you be home tonight* ______________________?

   No, I won't.

2. ______________________?

   Yes, I have.

3. ______________________?

   No, we couldn't.

4. ______________________?

   No, they didn't.

5. ______________________?

   No, I don't have to.

7b Questions with Wh- Words

Student Book p. 153

5 Practice

Match the questions with the answers about the Taj Mahal.

_____	**1.** How many workers built it?	**a.** Yes, it did.
_____	**2.** Who built it?	**b.** 1631.
_____	**3.** When did his wife die?	**c.** No, it isn't.
_____	**4.** Is the Taj Mahal in Afghanistan?	**d.** About 20,000.
_____	**5.** Did it take 22 years to build?	**e.** Shah Jahan.

6 Practice

Write questions based on the answers about the ancient African city of Timbuktu.

1. ____?

It's in Mali, near the Niger River. (where)

2. ____?

It was invaded by Morocco in 1593. (who)

3. ____?

It was famous for gold trade. (what)

4. ____?

In the 15th and 16th centuries it was a famous educational center. (when)

5. ________________________

________________________?

There was a university and about 100 schools for the Koran. (what)

6. ________________________

________________________?

Today it's an important meeting center for people in the Sahara. (why)

7 Practice

Write questions based on the answers about emperor penguins.

1. *What are emperor penguins?*

   Emperor penguins are <u>the biggest penguins in the penguin family</u>. (what)

2. ____?

   They are sometimes almost half the size of an adult human and <u>can weigh up to about 65 pounds</u>. (how much)

3. ____?

   They live on the <u>continent of Antarctica</u>. (where)

4. ____?

   They are <u>black and have yellow and white feathers near the neck</u>. (what)

5. ____?

   The female lays <u>one egg a year</u> and then leaves the egg with the father while she goes off to sea. (how many)

6. ____?

   ____?

   <u>The male</u> keeps the egg warm on his feet and covers it with his stomach for 65 days, in <u>the middle of winter</u>! (who) (when)

7. ____?

   When the baby hatches, the male feeds it <u>until the female returns</u>. Then it's his turn to go look for food. (how long)

7c Questions with *Who* and *What* as the Subject

Student Book p. 156

8 Practice

Read the story about a surprise party. Then ask and answer the questions with *who* or *what*.

Emily and Kyle went to a surprise party for their next-door neighbor, Roberto, but it was a disaster! Roberto's wife, Maria, was nervous and busy. Maria had invited all Roberto's friends, but not many people came. Roberto's mother, Mrs. Garcia, was there, but she wasn't happy. Mrs. Garcia told Maria that Maria hadn't prepared enough food and that her house wasn't clean enough. Then Maria and Roberto's dog, Marko, ate the birthday cake. Finally, Roberto came home, but he had a cold and didn't feel well.

1. ____________ went to the surprise party?

____.

2. ____________ was nervous and busy?

____.

3. ____________ is Mrs. Garcia?

____.

4. ____________ did Mrs. Garcia tell her daughter-in-law?

____.

5. ____________ happened to the birthday cake?

____.

6. ____________ was sick?

____.

9 Practice

Read the story about a fight. Then ask and answer the questions with *who* or *what*.

Bruno woke up suddenly at 3:30 in the morning. His neighbors were screaming very loudly. He heard a crash. He called the police. The police arrived and talked to Bruno's neighbors, Ed Bronson and Emily Craig. Mr. Bronson told the police that he had tripped over a rug and fallen. He had cut his forehead and broken his arm.

1. ____________ heard the screaming?

____.

2. ____________ did he hear?

____.

3. ____________ called the police?

____.

4. ____________ did he say?

____.

5. ____________ was hurt?

____.

6. ______________ happened?

____.

7. ______________did Mr. Bronson fall over?

____.

10 Practice

Complete the sentences with *who* or *what*.

A. Someone knocking at a door:

Jim: ______________ 's there?
(1)

Sarah: It's me.

Jim: ______________ do you want?
(2)

Sarah: May I use your phone?

B. Hakim, a businessman, missed his flight because he didn't have the right flight number or time. Now he's at the airport talking to his office.

Tom: ______________ happened?
(1)

Hakim: I missed my plane. ______________ (2) made the plans? ______________ (3) bought this ticket?

Tom: Our Los Angles office. I'll call them right now. ______________ (4) are you going to do?

Hakim: I'll try to get another flight.

C. Young: ______________ was at the party?
(1)

Choi: Irene, Kevin, Sachiko, Nikki, and David.

Young: ______________ did you do?
(2)

Choi: We talked and ate some snacks. Then we went out. ______________ (3) did you do?

Young: Nothing.

7d Questions with *Which* and *What*

Student Book p. 158

11 Practice

Complete the sentences with *which* or *what*.

A. Nancy: ______________ (1) is your major?

James: Chemistry.

Nancy: That's mine, too. ______________ (2) classes are you taking?

James: Intro to chemistry and some general education classes.

Nancy: ______________ (3) teacher do you have, Dr. Fredrick or Dr. Saunders?

James: I have Saunders.

Nancy: ______________ (4) book are you using, *Fundamentals* or *General Introduction*?

James: We're using a new book this semester, but I forget the name.

B. Peggy: ______________ (1) suitcase are you taking, the small black one or the old cloth one?

Duncan: I think I'll take the black one. ______________ (2) tie looks better, the blue one or the red one?

Peggy: I like the red one. Do you know ______________ (3) suit you're going to wear for the interview?

Duncan: I think the dark gray one.

C. Jun: ______________ (1) 's your favorite food?

Beth: I love Italian food.

Jun: ______________ (2) restaurant is your favorite?

Beth: I really like Lorenzo's on Main Street.

Jun: ______________ (3) do you usually order?

Beth: I usually get the linguini and clams.

D. Chie: _______________'s your favorite holiday? (1)

Doug: I love New Year's.

Chie: _______________ do you usually do? (2)

Doug: We visit our cousins.

Chie: _______________ cousins? The ones near you or the ones across town? (3)

Doug: We see both.

Chie: _______________ do you eat? (4)

Doug: Oh, my mom cooks a lot of great food.

E. Kim: I really like those earrings over there.

Sales clerk: _______________ ones, the silver ones or the gold ones?

F. Martin: Those desserts look really good!

Maureen: Let's get one.

Martin: _______________ one should we get? (1)

Maureen: Let's get the chocolate cake and the pie, and we can share them.

Waiter: That's a very good choice. _______________ would you like to drink? (2)

G. Scott: Let's meet at the coffee shop.

Frank: _______________ one? (1)

Scott: The one next to the campus bookstore.

Frank: Okay, _______________ time? (2)

Scott: About 7:00.

H. Principal: I need to talk to you about one of your students.

Teacher: _______________ one? (1)

Principal: The young man in the corner over there.

Teacher: Why? _______________ happened? (2)

12 Practice

Write answers to the questions.

1. Which day of the week is your favorite?

____.

2. What's your favorite color?

____.

3. Which hand do you write with?

____.

4. Which season is your favorite?

____.

5. Which parent are you closer to?

____.

6. What languages do you speak?

____.

7e Questions with *How*

Student Book p. 160

13 Practice

Complete the sentences with *how, how long, how many, how far, how much,* or *how often.*

A. Jarod and his family have just moved into a new house, and Jarod is talking to his new neighbor.

New neighbor: ____________ (1) did you live in your old house?

Jarod: We were there about ten years, but it was too small and a little far from my job. We needed more room because we have dogs.

New neighbor: ____________ (2) dogs do you have?

Jarod: We have three.

New neighbor: Where do you work?

Jarod: I work at Westco.

New neighbor: Really, ______________ (3) is it?

Jarod: Not far. I can ride my bike to work.

New neighbor: ______________ (4) about your wife? Does she work?

Jarod: Yes, she's a musician. She plays piano at some of the local jazz clubs.

New neighbor: ______________ (5) does she play?

Jarod: She usually plays three times a week.

B. Friends are lost.

Wendy: ______________ (1) is it?

Delores: I'm not sure.

Wendy: ______________ (2) do we get there?

Delores: I don't know. I think we're lost.

Wendy: ______________ (3) gas do we have?

Delores: We have enough.

Wendy: Let's ask that woman over there.

Delores: Okay, excuse me. ______________ (4) miles is it to the beach?

Woman: You're close. Just turn around and go back. Take a right at the light.

C. Sheila: What a wonderful costume! ______________ (1) did you make it?

Diana: Thanks. I found the directions on the Internet. It was easy.

Sheila: Was the material expensive? Can I ask you ______________ (2) it cost?

Diana: It was pretty cheap.

14 Practice

Complete the questions. Note that some questions with *how* are considered impolite.

1. Tim: ______________ old are you?

Victoria: That's none of your business!

2. Beth: ______________ do you weigh?

Janice: That's a rude question!

3. Jong: ______________ money do you make?

Fran: I can't believe you're asking me that. Didn't your parents teach you that that's a rude question?

15 Practice

Take a trivia quiz! Match the questions with the answers.

	Questions		Answers
____	**1.** Which country eats the most chocolate every year?	**a.**	Zacharias Janssen
____	**2.** What's the capital of Egypt?	**b.**	H_2O
____	**3.** How many time zones are there in the world?	**c.**	Switzerland—22 pounds/year/person
____	**4.** What's the chemical symbol for water?	**d.**	India
____	**5.** Who invented the microscope?	**e.**	South Africa
____	**6.** What country consumes the most tea?	**f.**	24
____	**7.** What country produces the most gold?	**g.**	Cairo

16 Practice

Complete the silly jokes. Read the first part of each joke. It asks a question. Try to answer it in a funny way. Your teacher has possible answers.

1. Three frogs are sitting on a lily pad. One decides to jump. How many are left?

   ______________________________.

2. What animal can jump higher than a house?

   ______________________________.

3. Why do birds fly south for the winter?

   ______________________________.

4. What time is it when an elephant sits on your fence?

   ______________________________.

5. Where does Friday come before Thursday?

   ______________________________.

6. How many elephants can fit in your car?

   ______________________________.

7f Tag Questions

Student Book p. 165

17 Practice

Write *C* next to the sentence if the tag question is correct. Write *I* if the tag question is incorrect.

_____ **1.** He's the boss, isn't it?

_____ **2.** Laura and Mike weren't there, were they?

_____ **3.** It's cold today, isn't it?

_____ **4.** You're from Mexico, are you?

_____ **5.** I'm included, aren't I?

_____ **6.** Kyle hasn't left, didn't he?

_____ **7.** They'll be there, will they?

_____ **8.** Sam didn't sleep well, did he?

_____ **9.** It wasn't what you expected, wasn't it?

_____ **10.** Catlin doesn't understand, does she?

18 Practice

Complete the sentences with the correct tag question.

1. Melissa is in a bad mood, ____________________?

2. Kate doesn't like spinach, ____________________?

3. I'm coming too, ____________________?

4. We don't have time for coffee, ____________________?

5. It's hot today, ____________________?

6. This test isn't hard, ____________________?

7. You've been to Chicago, ____________________?

8. They need to study more, ____________________?

9. Alice wears glasses, ____________________?

10. Mr. Daniels didn't get the message, ____________________?

11. We should go now, ______________________________?

12. You haven't eaten yet, ______________________________?

13. Our parents will meet us at the hotel, ______________________________?

14. Tag questions are easy, ______________________________?

15. We're finished, ______________________________?

19 Practice

Complete the conversations with the correct tag questions and short answers.

A. Rose: You're not listening, ______________________________?
1

Tina: I don't have a choice, ______________________________?
2

Rose: You don't care, ______________________________?
3

Tina: Yes, ______________. But you're always right, ______________?
4 5

B. Adam: You're going, ______________________________?
1

Patricia: No, ______________________________.
2

Adam: Why?

Patricia: I took some medicine.

Adam: You're not sick, ______________________________?
3

Patricia: Yes, ______________________________. A little.
4

20 Practice

Emile is studying for a science test. His older brother Walter is helping him. Complete the conversation with the correct tag questions and short answers.

Emile: Elephants can swim, ______________________________?
1

Walter: Yes, ______________________________.
2

Emile: Penguins don't fly, ______________________________?
3

Walter: No, ______________________________.
4

Emile: The sun is 93 million miles away, ______________________________?
5

Walter: Yes, ______________________________.
6

Emile: The longest river in the world is the Amazon,

______________________________?
7

Walter: No, ______________________ (8). The Nile is the longest river.

Emile: Bombay is in Pakistan, ______________________ (9)?

Walter: No, ______________________ (10). It's in India.

Emile: Galileo was Italian, ______________________ (11)?

Walter: Yes, ______________________ (12).

Emile: He invented the microscope, ______________________ (13)?

Walter: No, ______________________ (14). That was Zacharias Janssen.

Emile: Dogs can't see in color, ______________________ (15)?

Walter: No, ______________________ (16).

7g Phrasal Verbs

Student Book p. 167

21 Practice

Read the sentences. Write *T* next to the sentence if the phrasal verb is transitive. Write *I* if the phrasal verb is intransitive.

_____ **1.** They haven't gotten up yet.

_____ **2.** I'll call him back later.

_____ **3.** Mom came across my old high school photos in the attic.

_____ **4.** I hope the car doesn't break down.

_____ **5.** Please don't wake up the baby.

_____ **6.** I always stay up late working.

_____ **7.** We'll go over phrasal verbs one more time before the test.

_____ **8.** I ran into my ex-boyfriend at the movies.

_____ **9.** Could you look after my dog this weekend?

_____ **10.** They got back late last night.

7h Intransitive Phrasal Verbs

Student Book p. 168

22 Practice

Write *C* next to the sentence if the phrasal verb is correct. Write *I* if the phrasal verb is incorrect.

_____ **1.** Let's sit down them.

_____ **2.** The people stood up when the judge entered the courtroom.

_____ **3.** Xavier has a headache. He's lying down.

_____ **4.** The Feins set out it late yesterday morning.

_____ **5.** Smitty's motorcycle broke down in front of the bank.

_____ **6.** Vivian wants to stay up to watch the eclipse of the moon.

_____ **7.** We got up them at 6:00.

_____ **8.** When did you get back it?

23 Practice

Circle the correct phrasal verb.

1. If you don't feel well, (stand up / lie down).

2. Another way to say *return* is (go back / get up).

3. My back hurts. I need to (set out / stand up).

4. Sophia wants to go to the play, but it doesn't start until 10:00. She's going to (stay up / sit down) late.

5. My grandfather (gets up / breaks down) at 4:30 in the morning.

24 Practice

Write answers to the following questions.

1. On the bus, do you prefer to stand up or sit down? ______________________________.

Why? ____.

2. Do you like to stay up late or get up early? ______________________________.

Why? ____.

3. When do you prefer to set out on vacation, in the early morning or later in the day?

______________________________. Why? ______________________________.

7i Transitive Phrasal Verbs: Separable

Student Book p. 171

25 Practice

Circle the correct phrasal verb. Then rewrite the sentences, changing the position of the objects.

1. Madelyn, please (pick up / look up) your clothes.
2. If you don't want those old papers, (throw them away / wake them up).
3. Jessica (turned on / called back) her MP3 player.
4. Rob needs to (look up / fill out) the application.
5. Rick, you said you were on a diet. (Put down / Put off) the ice cream cone, and move slowly away from the table.

1. *Madelyn, please pick your clothes up*.
2. ______________________________.
3. ______________________________.
4. ______________________________.
5. ______________________________.

26 Practice

Complete the sentences with phrasal verbs from the list and the objects in parentheses.

call back	pick up	throw out	wake up
look up	put off	turn on	write down

Ms. Jarvis is meeting Mr. Harris, a very important client, today. She's discussing plans for the meeting with her assistant, David Harn.

Ms. Jarvis: David, please (the schedule) ___(1)___ for me.

David: Sure.

Ms. Jarvis: Could you please (my other appointments) ___(2)___ until next week? I'm going to be very busy today. I'd like to take a nap, so please (me) ___(3)___ at 1:30. Who is (Mr. Harris) ___(4)___ at the airport?

David: We sent a limousine.

Ms. Jarvis: Good. Could you please (the numbers) ___(5)___ of some of the other people in his office? I may need to call them later.

David: Of course. By the way, you got a call from Richmond Brothers.

Ms. Jarvis: I'll (them) ____________ (6) tomorrow. The conference room is very warm, and it's not cleaned up.

David: I'll (the air conditioning) ____________ (7) and (any trash) ____________ (8) that's in the room.

Ms. Jarvis: Thanks, David.

27 Practice

Write as many things as you can for each category.

1. Things that you throw out

a. ____________

b. ____________

c. ____________

2. Things you put off

a. ____________

b. ____________

c. ____________

3. Things you pick up

a. ____________

b. ____________

c. ____________

4. Things you look up

a. ____________

b. ____________

c. ____________

5. Things you fill out

a. ____________

b. ____________

c. ____________

6. Things you turn on

   a. ______________________________

   b. ______________________________

   c. ______________________________

7j Transitive Phrasal Verbs: Inseparable

Student Book p. 175

28 Practice

Circle the correct phrasal verb.

1. Joe had a terrible cold, but he (got over / came across) it.
2. Theresa (got out / ran into) her English teacher at the theater.
3. Everyone had to (get off / get into) the bus and wait for another one.
4. She's (going over / looking after) the recipe one more time before we start baking.
5. A nanny is someone who (looks after / looks into) children.
6. I was late because I (got on / got over) the wrong bus.
7. Employee: My check was wrong.

   Boss: I'll (run into / look into) it.
8. George was cleaning out his backpack and (got into / came across) an old letter from 2003.

29 Practice

Write *C* next to the sentence if the phrasal verb is used correctly. Write *I* if the phrasal verb is used incorrectly. Some phrasal verbs are separable and some are inseparable.

_____ 1. Nurses look the patients after.

_____ 2. She put it off until next week.

_____ 3. I didn't pick it up. It was dirty.

_____ 4. My little sister ran the neighbors into at the grocery store.

_____ 5. We looked into it.

_____ 6. Karl turned it off before he went to bed.

SELF-TEST

A Choose the best answer, A, B, C, or D, to complete the sentence. Mark your answer by darkening the oval with the same letter.

1. Jan: _______ 's your homework?
Andreas: On the desk.

A. Who (A) (B) (C) (D)
B. Where
C. What
D. When

2. _______ money does he have?

A. How many (A) (B) (C) (D)
B. How about
C. How much
D. How

3. Mom's really tired. She's going to _______.

A. lie down (A) (B) (C) (D)
B. get up
C. go over
D. stand up

4. He's a teacher, _______?

A. he isn't (A) (B) (C) (D)
B. isn't he
C. he is
D. he's

5. _______ were you talking to?

A. Where (A) (B) (C) (D)
B. What
C. When
D. Who

6. Have your parents retired yet? _______

A. Yes, they are. (A) (B) (C) (D)
B. No, they didn't.
C. Yes, they did.
D. Yes, they have.

7. She doesn't smoke, _______?

A. does she (A) (B) (C) (D)
B. doesn't she
C. she doesn't
D. she does

8. The milk is really old. _______

A. Throw out it. (A) (B) (C) (D)
B. Put it on.
C. Throw it out.
D. Put it off.

9. _______ one did you pick?

A. What (A) (B) (C) (D)
B. Which
C. How
D. Where

10. Your brother can drive, _______?

A. can he (A) (B) (C) (D)
B. he can
C. he can't
D. can't he

B Find the underlined word or phrase, A, B, C, or D, that is incorrect. Mark your answer by darkening the oval with the same letter.

1. You didn't (A) look (B) up it (C), did you (D)?

Ⓐ Ⓑ Ⓒ Ⓓ

2. Who (A) happened to the store (B) on (C) the corner (D)?

Ⓐ Ⓑ Ⓒ Ⓓ

3. She'll met (A) us (B) there, won't (C) she (D)?

Ⓐ Ⓑ Ⓒ Ⓓ

4. The artist (A) paint (B) landscape paintings (C), didn't he (D)?

Ⓐ Ⓑ Ⓒ Ⓓ

5. We didn't (A) wake up (B) it (C) early this morning, did we (D)?

Ⓐ Ⓑ Ⓒ Ⓓ

6. Our class (A) went over (B) the questions, didn't (C) I (D)?

Ⓐ Ⓑ Ⓒ Ⓓ

7. Who (A) is the teacher going to (B) hand back (C) the tests (D)?

Ⓐ Ⓑ Ⓒ Ⓓ

8. How much (A) times did (B) we (C) talk (D) about this?

Ⓐ Ⓑ Ⓒ Ⓓ

9. When (A) was waiting (B) for Kate after (C) school this afternoon (D)?

Ⓐ Ⓑ Ⓒ Ⓓ

10. The team has won (A) the championship every year for (B) the past five years (C), has it (D)?

Ⓐ Ⓑ Ⓒ Ⓓ